To Roger with all
Good Wishes for birthday
19th Dec/70.

M. S.

PORTRAIT OF THE PENNINES

THE *PORTRAIT* SERIES

By the same author
Rambles in the Hebrides
Rambles in Peakland
Rambles in North Wales

Portrait of
THE PENNINES

ROGER A. REDFERN

ILLUSTRATED
WITH PHOTOGRAPHS BY
E. HECTOR KYME
AND WITH MAP

ROBERT HALE · LONDON

SBN 7091 0872 9

Robert Hale & Company
63 Old Brompton Road
London S.W.7

PRINTED IN GREAT BRITAIN
BY EBENEZER BAYLIS AND SON, LTD.
THE TRINITY PRESS, WORCESTER, AND LONDON

CONTENTS

ILLUSTRATIONS

ACKNOWLEDGEMENTS

ALL the photographs in this book are the work of my friend E. Hector Kyme, to whom I am greatly indebted. He is celebrated as a photographer-artist, though not as well known as he deserves; I hope that this book will help to improve matters in that direction.

The Pennines are not the easiest subject for successful photography. They are not, generally speaking, shapely like many of the mountains of Lakeland, Snowdonia and western Scotland and so need the eye of an artist and the technique of a first-class photographer to do them justice. To reduce the number of photographs from the scores taken to those I have been able to include has been a difficult and a heartless task.

I had the pleasure of accompanying Hector when he took most of these photographs, an experience that produced some amusing as well as enlightening situations. "Stop this car instantly!" was his cry as we passed a particularly attractive cottage in Langstrothdale. Then there was the moment which rarely happens twice in a lifetime, as a southbound freight train crossed the Ribblehead Viaduct just as the sun was setting, and we had but a second or two to stop the car. E. H. K. jumped out and exposed the film, hoping that shutter speed and depth of focus were correct. Subsequent events proved that they had been, as can be seen later in this book. These Pennine days have been "a feast", morsels of which are reproduced here.

For those who are interested, the following data will be useful:

Camera: Yashica D (2¼ins. square)
Film: FP3
Developer: Promicrol

I am also greatly indebted to Mrs. W. Craig for the efficient way in which she has typed and read the manuscript and helped compile the index, so relieving me of a large burden; and to Mrs.

P. J. Bunker, Secretary of the Inland Waterways Protection Society, for many of the details of Pennine canals contained in Chapter II. And I wish to thank the Editor of *Country Life*, Mr. John Adams, for permission to reproduce an article of mine which originally appeared in that magazine in the chapter on the Sheep of Peakland.

R. A. R.

CHAPTER I

THE BACKBONE OF NORTHERN ENGLAND

ALONG the lane near my home long ago, when I was a small child, the Pennines appeared as a line of blue hills; the backcloth to my westward-facing world. Blue hills rolling with gentle horizons under a midsummer's evening sky, purple on autumn afternoons, and high, white mountains when winter snowfall was followed by crisp, anticyclonic days.

In later years those eastern undulations of the southern Pennines, ups-and-downs, folds and escarpments rounded by time, were an inevitable obstacle, to be cycled up with tired legs and bursting lungs before the wild country of the high moors was reached. How many cyclists have had thunder in their minds as they laboured up the Pennine flanks from the industrial east and west?

"Over the moors" was, and still is, a common phrase in my part of the country. It simply means on to, into or across the Pennine heights, the wild moors which open out beyond Owler Bar and Fox House. Moorland which is part of the Peak District, that fine and final downthrust of upland which stretches to the Scottish border as the Pennines.

Pennine Chain, Pennine Range, the Backbone of England—call it what you will—it is basically a ridge cast up in geological time by great pressures on the earth's crust in this area. The name Pennine is probably derived from the Celtic 'pen' meaning 'high'. The word appears in Appenines and Pennine Alps. Subsequently the great ridge has been subjected to erosion from all the natural forces and is no longer quite so simple in form as it originally was. Nevertheless, the north-south trend is obvious, and so is the main watershed and the various strata of which the ridge is composed.

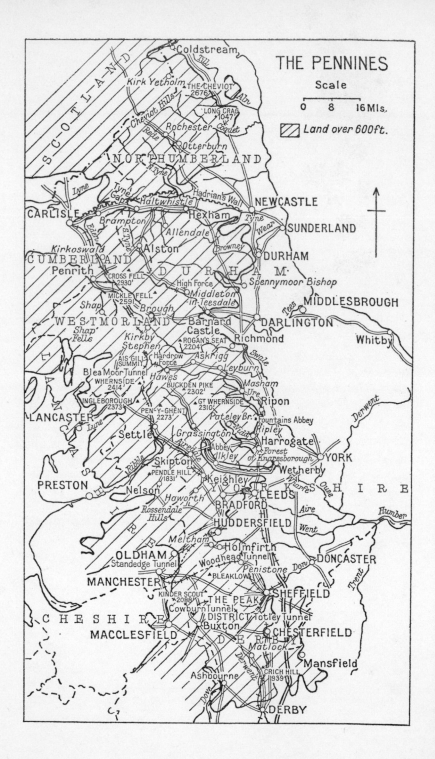

THE PENNINES

Scale

0   8   16 Mls.

///// Land over 600ft.

Coldstream
Kirk Yetholm
THE CHEVIOT
2676
Cheviot Hills
LONG CRAG
1047
Rochester
Coquet
Otterburn
N.Tyne
NORTHUMBERLAND
Till
Aln
Rede

SCOTLAND

Tyne
Tyne
Gap
Haltwhistle
Hadrian's Wall
NEWCASTLE
CARLISLE
Hexham
Tyne
SUNDERLAND
Brampton
Eden
Allendale
Wear
Kirkoswald
Alston
Browney
DURHAM
CUMBERLAND
Penrith
D U R H A M
Spennymoor Bishop
CROSS FELL
2930'
High Force
MICKLE FELL
2591'
Middleton
in Teesdale
MIDDLESBROUGH
Shap
Brough
Tees
DARLINGTON
WESTMORLAND
Barnard
Castle
Whitby
Shap'
Fells
Kirkby
Stephen
ROGAN'S SEAT
2204'
Richmond
AIS GILL
SUMMIT
Hardrow
Force
Askrigg
Swale
Blea Moor Tunnel
Hawes
Leyburn
WHERNSIDE
2414
BUCKDEN PIKE
2302'
Masham
INGLEBOROUGH
2373'
GT WHERNSIDE
2310'
Ure
Ripon
LANCASTER
PEN-Y-GHENT
2273'
Pateley Br.
Derwent
Tyne
Settle
Grassington
Fountains Abbey
Ripley
Harrogate
Skipton
Abbey
Ilkley
Forest
of Knaresborough
YORK
PENDLE HILL
1831'
Keighley
Wharfe
Ouse
PRESTON
Nelson
Y O R K S H I R E
Wetherby
Ribble
LEEDS
Haworth
BRADFORD
Aire
Humber
Rossendale
Hills
HUDDERSFIELD
Went
Meltham
Holmfirth
OLDHAM
Standedge Tunnel
Woodhead Tunnel
Penistone
Don
DONCASTER
MANCHESTER
BLEAKLOW
KINDER SCOUT
2088
THE PEAK
SHEFFIELD
Trent
CHESHIRE
Cowburn Tunnel
DISTRICT
Totley Tunnel
CHESTERFIELD
MACCLESFIELD
Buxton
D E R B.
Matlock
Mansfield
Derwent
CRICH HILL
1939'
Ashbourne
Dove
DERBY

So what better place than here to take a brief look at the structure of these uplands.

The structure is basically monoclinal, with rocks tilted slightly towards the east and cut off on the western side by sharp down-folding and by faulting. The greatest period of earth movements was during Hercynian times, after the great depths of limestone, millstone grit and coal measures had been deposited during the Carboniferous period. The great dome or anticline of the Howgill Fells was formed at the height of these earth movements. This dome was isolated from a great block of unfolded rocks known as the Askrigg massif by a zone of complicated faulting called the Dent Line. In fact, the unchanged Askrigg massif is edged to the west by this Dent Line and to the south by the well-known Craven Faults.

It is in this district of the Craven faults, where the Carboni-ferous limestone abuts against the millstone grit, that the very oldest rocks of the Pennines are located. Here pre-Cambrian rocks occur in one or two places, as at Chapel le Dale and Horton in Ribblesdale, where slates with bands of grit and conglomerate are found and known as 'Ingleton granite'. It has been shown that these very ancient rocks closely resemble the Longmyndian rocks of Salop, no fossils ever having been found up to the present time. In a boring two miles east of Buxton volcanic rocks of the Uriconian type were discovered between 900 and 1,024 feet below the sur-face, and the deepest well of the Nottinghamshire oilfields (7,476 feet) reached down into quartzites which are presumed to be of pre-Cambrian origin.

It is upon the great platform of these oldest rocks that the well-known materials of the Pennines were deposited, consolidated and uplifted—the limestone, more recent millstone grit and even younger coal measures (all of Carboniferous age) overlie each other respectively. The later uplifting caused the great ridge which is the major feature of the present-day Pennines, a ridge which reached a considerable altitude and has subsequently been denuded by the combined action of the many agents of erosion, not least by the force of falling waters.

This erosion has been at various rates so that different rocks lie exposed beneath Pennine skies, resulting in different scenic features and varying patterns of settlement, agriculture and industry. Carboniferous limestone is the surface material over much of the Askrigg massif in the north and down to the famous Craven district. In this northern section, too, there occur the well-known 'Yoredale Beds'— a mixture of shales, sandstones and limestone giving rise to "a broad-featured country of step-topography and waterfalls". These 'beds' are well seen in the slopes of several notable heights which rise above the general plateau surface of the Askrigg massif; heights which include Ingleborough, Whernside and Penygent.

To the south of Craven, between Skipton and the Peak District, are the central Pennines, and these are characterized by "moors and peat-mosses, with crags and edges and stony cloughs descending to deep landslip-cumbered valleys"; this is the typical gritstone country, where millstone grit is king.

This gritstone country sweeps right down into Peakland and virtually surrounds the older limestone, lying exposed again in the 'White Peak' which occupies a good proportion of central and western Derbyshire.

On both sides of the gritstone country of the central and southern Pennines lie the younger coal measures forming the Lancashire and Yorkshire, Nottinghamshire and Derbyshire coalfields. From the densely populated and dirty towns which have arisen in both these areas have come the people who first discovered the freedom of the hills "just beyond their back gardens, at the top of their street". The rambling movements before World War I started on both sides of the southern Pennines and grew greatly between the wars so that today this ridge, this infinitely varied hill country is the roaming ground of thousands, a wilderness and sanctuary for the mind.

The Pennines are not desolate and forlorn; they are infinitely rich in varied scenery and weather, in flora and fauna. The very variety which characterizes the geological structure of the ridge has resulted in a similar variety of scenery and uses of that scenery:

> From Cheviot crests to Edale slopes,
> On gritstone scarps with nylon ropes;

White-coated hares in winter
And cloudberries in the sun.

Long-legged walks in lowering clouds
On peaty plateaux far from crowds.
Dry valleys and white-washed coves
And chasms of the deep
Where living waters sleep
Before the downhill plunge
To Humber, Lune and Ribble sands.

Yes indeed, the very charm of these hills is the variety to be
found in the 250 miles of them. A January night on Cross Fell,
with a full moon on the drifted snow, and a June midday above
Malham Cove have more than a little in common, for the
predominant colour (if moonlight is allowed to show colour)
is white, though the details are very different. Then again, a walk
up Ingleborough is a very different thing from a walk along
Dovedale in high summer; or a look at a high-Pennine farm
like Mossylee, above Glossop, is a very different experience from
a look at a farm in lower Wharfedale or in Cordwell Valley at
the eastern edge of Peakland. All is Pennine, but within that
sphere is a whole world of differences.

In the following chapters we will look at some of the various
characteristics and characters which go towards making Pennine
country.

CHAPTER II

OVER AND UNDER

THE Pennines have always presented a formidable barrier to transport, and the only saving grace was that the watershed ran roughly from north to south, and in former times (as now) most of the important routes ran in that same direction and could run across the eastern and western lowlands to either side *en route* to Scotland or the Midlands and London.

With the dawn of industrialization on both sides of the ridge the need arose for better communications between Cumberland and Northumberland, between Lancashire and Yorkshire. The old drovers' and shepherds' tracks would no longer suffice; cotton, wool and woollen products, iron products and coal had to traverse the breadth of northern England, and so new ways across were devised.

The Tyne Gap, the low trough between east and west drained by the south Tyne River to the North Sea and by the River Irthing to the Eden and Solway Firth, really marks the northern limit of the Pennines; beyond is Cheviot-land. This trough is used by the main line between Newcastle-upon-Tyne and Carlisle, which has to climb only to approximately 500 feet above sea-level in the section between Haltwhistle and Brampton in the vicinity of Mains Rigg and Gilsland.

The next line to cross the main watershed is that of the former London and North Eastern Railway, a double track which was constructed from Barnard Castle to Tebay on the main London, Midland and Scottish Railway Company's line south of Shap. This climbs up the valley of the River Greta, a tributary of the Tees, and reaches 1,400 feet at Black Riggs close to the remains of

16

the Roman fortlet known as Maiden Castle. The line then descends deviously above the valley of the River Belah and so close to Kirkby Stephen in the Eden Valley. Surprisingly enough the engineers of this route managed without a tunnel of any length. It is interesting to notice the closeness of the Roman road (followed closely by the present A66 route between Richmond and Brough) to the railway across the highest land of Stainmore Forest. This is the famous Stainmore Summit so well known to railway enthusiasts, a pass almost as high as the 1,484 feet Druimuachdar Summit in Scotland—the highest stretch of railway in Britain.

Two roads lead out of the head of lovely Swaledale. One, towards the north-west and over by Birk Dale, reaching 1,698 feet above sea-level on Lamps Moss. It is an unfenced road which winds typically over the heights and down into the Vale of Eden. The other is the lane which breaks off the main dale-road at the village of Thwaite and climb southwards above the Cliff Beck and so down into Wensleydale at Hardrow. This unfenced lane crosses the wild pass between Great Shunner Fell (2,340 feet) and Lovely Seat (2,213 feet). This 1,726-foot pass is the famous Butter Tubs, with the pot-holes known as the Butter Tubs close by the road. Both routes are relics of very ancient tracks which were used primarily by farmers, drovers and travelling tradesmen. The surface of these routes has slowly been improved over the years of this century.

The Midland Railway Company built their main line from London to Carlisle and Scotland during the middle years of the nineteenth century. The section of the line between Derby and Leeds was built in 1840. The route then turned to the north-west, up the Aire valley; and by 1846 the ten and threequarter miles of rail between Leeds and Shipley were opened. By 1847 the line had been built as far as Skipton at the mouth of the Aire Gap, the most important depression across the width of the entire Pennines between the Tyne Gap in the north and the southern Peak District. The line then turned to the north, following the upper Ribble valley. From here the engineers had the overwhelming problem of negotiating the complex and high terrain at the head

2

Tan Hill Inn

of the Ribble, the Greta and the Ure in order to get into the Eden Valley, which leads relatively easily down to Carlisle.

The section of the line beyond Skipton was completed as far as Settle in the Ribble Valley by 1849, but it was not until twenty-six years later—1875—that the line was built on to its destination at Carlisle. What were some of the difficulties which made progress so comparatively slow to the north of Settle?

For six miles the line followed the floor of the narrowing Ribblesdale, as far as the village of Horton in Ribblesdale; then it was built over the eastern flanks of Park Fell, reaching 1,050 feet at Ribblehead Station. Beyond this the low ground drained by the River Greta at the upper end of the valley had to be traversed by a high viaduct (the Ribblehead Viaduct), which slowed down progress even further. Now high ground confronted the engineers, the 2,419-foot summit of Whernside, Blea Moor and Gayle Moor. The line was continued up the narrowing confines of Little Dale into the heart of wild Blea Moor until progress on the surface became impracticable. The notorious Blea Moor Tunnel was commenced, and for a long period Man struggled with Nature to make a safe route through the heart of the Pennines, an underground route of 2,629 yards, which has its northern portal at Mossy Bottom at the very head of Dentdale. Instability of the rock strata led to many rock falls during the construction work of the tunnel, and work had already been seriously delayed when water seepage led to flooding. Pumps carried the water away, but still the moor above poured down its hidden reservoir of ground water, and at one time there was even thought of abandoning the tunnel in favour of another route. To this day Blea Moor Tunnel is notorious for the amount of time and labour required on maintenance work.

The line contoured around the head of lovely Dentdale, of scattered farms and stone walled fields, assisted on its way by many cuttings and embankments, into the head of Cowgill Beck and so through a three-quarter-mile tunnel beneath Rise Hill-end, which was excavated through solid rock to reach the upper end of Garsdale, and so across the slight watershed to the head of Wensleydale at Hawes Junction, (now known as Garsdale), where the single track line winding up this dale from Askrigg and beyond came in. A steady climb of three miles now lay ahead, to the head of the pass leading over and down into the upper Eden Valley known as Mallerstang Common. This pass is known to railway enthusiasts the world over as Ais Gill Summit and reaches 1,169 feet above sea-level. M. W. Earley's fine photograph of a L.M.S.R. 4-4-0 three-cylinder compound locomotive hauling a 'banana special' over Ais Gill Summit in pre-war days, and appropriately entitled "In Banana Days", has always given me a thrill— steady, laboured progress on a sunny summer's day, with the high and shapely crest of Wild Boar Fell behind. This Midland Railway route, which became part of the L.M.S.R. in 1923, is full of character, and even today a journey behind a throbbing diesel locomotive is an exciting experience guaranteed to promote respect for the engineers who constructed the line between 1869 and 1876.

But perhaps the greatest single event for the Settle-Carlisle railway at least as regards the number of people gathered alongside the line throughout its entire length occurred on Sunday, 11th August, 1968. This was the date decided by the British Railways Board on which all steam-hauled trains would cease to run, the end of the great era which really began on 15th September, 1830, when the Liverpool-Manchester Railway was officially opened, a year after the famous steam locomotive trials at Rainhill between the two cities.

We were on that most scenic of all English railway routes where it climbs over and under the Pennines north of Ribblehead. The special train due to carry enthusiasts on the trip from Liverpool Lime Street to Carlisle and back called at Manchester and Burnley and was due to arrive at Ais Gill Summit at 1.45 p.m., where it would stop for twenty minutes for the passengers and the assembled lineside crowd to take photographs.

The morning dawned dry and warm, not a cloud in the sky, and when we arrived at Ais Gill many scores of cars were already parked. There was a holiday mood here and, with two hours to go before the last remaining 'Britannia' (Pacific 4-6-2 type) No. 70013 *Oliver Cromwell* was due to haul the special to a halt at this upland vantage point, many enthusiasts, young and old, were wandering over the main lines and examining the loop lines, cross-over and signal wire. This is the highest point on any British main line and the signal box here is normally one of the loneliest—today it was full to bursting with enthusiasts, police and railway officials!

Suddenly there was the distant whistle of a steam locomotive, and a pair of Stanier Class Fives came through running light, the engines which would be bringing the train back from Carlisle. They made a fitting introduction to the day's proceedings as they passed at speed.

The gangers came down the shallow cutting on to the track resplendent with orange pullovers, red and green flags and a black horn apiece. Quite soon two police officers with a loud hailer announced the imminent passing of the south-bound "Thames-Clyde" express and everyone was turned back behind the fence. As the last spectators retreated a ganger blew his horn three times, and the diesel-hauled train thundered through towards Settle and Leeds. The crowd increased and as zero hour approached we learnt that the train had just left Hellifield, where *Oliver Cromwell* had taken on water. It was already running late because of delay in getting sufficient water on board from the water column at Blackburn, which required the engine to be taken off the train and filled with 1,000 gallons from another column.

"It's just left Garsdale," the policeman shouted to the crowd, and everyone pressed a little nearer to the fencing—Garsdale is only three miles away down the bank. Time passed slowly, and we imagined that the delay must be due to slow running past all the hundreds of enthusiasts lining the route between Garsdale, Shotlock Tunnel and Ais Gill. At last, it must have been a quarter-of-an-hour after the train left Garsdale, a ganger's horn blew, and the great bulk of the Pacific engine slid—slowly and almost silently—up to the summit and stopped opposite the signal box. The crowd swept down on to the line as one man and was joined by most of the 470 passengers. Still camera shutters clicked, ciné-cameras whirred, and tape recorders were set in motion.

"Ais Gill has never seen anything like this before!" someone said as we crossed the main lines for the tenth time. I am sure they were right. The arrival of the first passenger train when the Settle-Carlisle route was opened on 1st May 1876 would not have seen a tenth of the crowd which brought the summit to life today. Because the train was thirty minutes behind schedule it only stopped for a quarter-of-an-hour. Then the guard's whistle blew, a loud hailer instructed the passengers to board the train immediately, and the locomotive's siren sounded. Jets of steam blasted along the track, and *Oliver Cromwell* moved off sedately, driving wheels spinning momentarily. Then the train was off, under the bridge and away down the upper Eden Valley. My last view of it was after a quick scramble to the nearby bridge parapet, where the already distant train was gathering speed, dominated by the great, shapely bulk of Wild Boar Fell. We would never again see such a plume of steam below that high Pennine hill as a train descended towards Carlisle.

We now drove the eleven miles southwards in order to see the train for the last time as it returned towards Liverpool. Perhaps the most scenically dramatic and beautiful stretch of the line is at Dent Head, where one can see the progress of a train as it comes southwards towards Blea Moor Tunnel's northern portal at Mossy Bottom. In the warm and sunny tranquility of that August tea-time we gathered on the cutting by the mouth of the usually dark and threatening tunnel. There was a feeling of mellowed melancholy, if there be quite such a thing. It was very hard to believe that it was almost all over, that never again should we see the spectacle of a British Railways' steam-hauled train. The bank on which we sat and chatted with fellow enthusiasts—there were only thirty or forty people about Mossy Bottom, in complete contrast to the hordes at Ais Gill—was pink with heather flowers, and across the line was a colony of rosebay willowherb in vivid bloom. We talked of 'Jubilees' which were no more—*Alberta*, *Straits Settlements* and the rest.

"She's coming, lads!" a man called from his wall-top perch, and there, sure enough, we could see the distant line of steam as the double-headed train sped around the 1,100 feet contour towards us. The sun gleamed upon Dent Fell and caught steam and paintwork in turn, then out of sight as it crossed Arten Gill Viaduct and entered the lengthy cutting protected by double rows of snow fencing. Again it came into view, passing the now-closed Dent Head signal-box and sweeping over Dent Head Viaduct. The rapid beat of the shining Stanier Class Fives grew louder, and then they were passing and as quickly had gone with shrill whistles blowing—into the black depths of Blea Moor. The last blue and cream coach sped out of sight, and all that was left for us to see was the blue-grey smoke curling up from Mossy Bottom into the clear air. We ran at top speed up the 390 feet to the northernmost ventilation shaft in the hope of getting a photograph of the last smoke and steam issuing out over the moor, but virtually none came. However, this excursion had two rewards. Firstly, there was the wonderful vista of upper Dentdale and the fells in every direction, dappled with cloud shadows. There was no sound up there in the warm sunlight, though by going close to the smoke-blackened brick chimney at the top of the ventilation shaft the eerie trickle of drainage water down the 390 feet to railway level could be plainly heard. So we went down again to Mossy Bottom, and as we took a last look at the blue-grey smoke still curling out of the portal the second reward came. There was a sudden distant whistle, that of a steam locomotive! We could see another plume of steam as a light engine passed through Dent Station and came along the line towards Dent Head. It was *Oliver Cromwell* returning to Manchester—the very last British Railways steam locomotive to use this line. Out of the cutting, over Dent Head Viaduct and on she came. There was little more than a whisper as the Pacific slid by, her green paintwork still shining in the lowering western sun. A wave from the fireman, and she was gone at 30 miles an hour under Blea Moor; no whistle this time, just the gentle motion of the valves and a final curtain of blue-grey smoke at Mossy Bottom.

No more will steam traction raise the echoes romantically on the fells. I, for one, will always miss the fascination which this finest of all mechanical inventions has added to all types of country in general and to the Pennines in particular.

The Leeds and Liverpool Canal was opened in 1816, after a construction period of forty-six years, and cost £1,200,000. It followed the course of the River Aire west of Leeds, never far from the railway line just mentioned. Perhaps the finest features of this section of the canal are the Five Locks at Bingley, forming a veritable 'ladder' and well seen from the railway line. The British Transport Commission's Board of Survey under the chairmanship of Lord Rusholme published their report on waterways in 1955. Among their proposals was that the Leeds and Liverpool Canal should be retained for transport purposes and encouragement given "to the development of traffic". To the west of the Pennines this canal winds through Burnley and Wigan and much of industrial Lancashire *en route* for Liverpool and the Mersey.

To the south of the last canal route the Rochdale Canal winds its shorter way over the Pennine watershed between the Calder valley and Rochdale and Manchester. This waterway was built by the notable engineer, John Rennie, and completed in 1804. It has been described as "typical of Rennie, with wide locks and a singular disregard for any natural obstacles". There were 92 locks in the length of 33 miles and the famous Samuel Smiles noted that "no more formidable difficulties, indeed, were encountered by George Stephenson, in constructing the railway passing by tunnel under the same range of hills than were overcome by Mr. Rennie." In 1953 the Rochdale Canal was abandoned, having been the first waterway to provide a through connection over the Pennines.

The third canal route over the Pennine watershed is the famous Huddersfield Narrow Canal, built by Samuel Outram and completed in 1811. Great difficulties were experienced in traversing the highest ground, including the construction of 74 locks in a distance of 20 miles and the great Standedge tunnel, which reaches 644 feet above sea-level. It is 3 miles and 135 yards long and is, in fact, the highest and longest waterway tunnel in Britain. Quite early in its history the canal came under railway control, and it is interesting to realize that the Standedge railway tunnel follows a parallel course to the canal tunnel, being the same length as the latter. Unfortunately for the users of the canal, subsequent to the construction of the adjoining railway tunnel a number of trans-

verse shafts were constructed to take away the smoke and steam.
This saved the trouble of constructing vertical ventilating shafts to
the surface but caused the canal tunnel to become regularly
choked by fumes. Mr. P. J. Bunker of the Inland Waterways Protection Society has recalled a memorable journey through this
famous underground waterway, when smoke belched through
the numerous transverse shafts from the railway tunnel; the lights
of passing trains were clearly visible—a unique subterranean
experience. In 1944 the Huddersfield Narrow was abandoned, a
retrograde step indeed, for this waterway had been and could
have remained a most valuable commercial route for the transport of heavy and valuable loads between the industrial conurbations of Lancashire and Yorkshire's West Riding. Could not
this route have been used, too, for pleasure cruises in summer,
taking visitors through wild country and giving interested parties
a leisurely view of an outstanding canal-engineering undertaking
of the nineteenth century? Today the Standedge canal tunnel is
not open to traffic, but the water remains, forming an essential
reservoir for those waterways which still operate on both sides of
the Pennines.

The Huddersfield and Manchester line of the former Lancashire and Yorkshire Railway Company (later to be absorbed
into the L.N.W.R., and still later, in 1923, to be absorbed into the
great L.M.S.R.) passed beneath the Pennines in the Standedge railway tunnel (3 miles and 62 yards) referred to above in connection
with the canal tunnel of the same name. This was the most direct
railway route between the West Riding's woollen towns and
Manchester. Over the surface the A62 road crosses the gritstone
moors between Huddersfield and Oldham, by way of Slaithwaite
and Marsden—where the famous walk to Edale in Peakland
begins. The road from Holmfirth to Oldham climbs over the
northern flanks of Black Hill and White Moss by the now-derelict
Isle of Skye Inn, one of the hostelries on the Four Inns Walk
across the southern Pennines. To the south the Great Central Railway wound up the upper valley of the River Don from Sheffield
to Penistone and so by Hazelhead to Dunford Bridge, where
tunnelling operations began a little way west of the station. This

is the famous Woodhead Tunnel with its twin tunnels, one for each track, measuring 3 miles and 17 yards long. This route was opened in 1845—an early date for so difficult a route. The western portals of the tunnels are at Woodhead Station, and photographs showing Great Central locomotives hauling trains and passing each other at these portals were once well known, clouds of dense smoke and steam at the approach to or exit from those eliptical mouths suggesting speed and great noise. Almost 1,500 people lived in or near these tunnels during its construction, and 60 men were killed and 200 severely injured during that time.

The two tunnels were actually bored between 1839 and 1852. The first one was completed by 1845 and was, at that time, the longest tunnel in the British Isles. It was during these years that 32 men were killed and 140 severely injured, but during the operations in connection with the second tunnel—between 1847 and 1852—an outbreak of cholera was responsible for the deaths of 28 men. Today one of these two tunnels is being adapted to carry high-voltage transmission cables beneath the Pennines so that it is still serving a useful purpose, and the moorland overhead remains relatively unspoilt.

In 1955 this line, which had become part of the L.N.E.R. system in 1923, was electrified, and a new tunnel, driven under the watershed immediately to the south of the old twin tunnels, was completed in 1954 after 6 years work and at an expense of £4¼ million. A high-speed journey through the clean and well-lit new tunnel emphasized the contrast with the black and ill-ventilated 'pits' adjoining. Banking engines were formerly needed behind most trains on the steep pull up from Sheffield to Dunford Bridge, and progress was slow and heavy on coal, especially on the Garratt engine. And now, after so short a time, plans are afoot to close this particular route to passenger traffic. Under goes the railway and over goes the Woodhead Pass, not much of a road pass really, for the route crosses from one side to the other almost at summit level due to the plateau-type nature of the terrain. This is an important trunk route (the A628) between Yorkshire's West Riding and South Lancashire, and a tremendous weight of heavy goods traffic goes over Woodhead. In bad winters the road regularly becomes blocked, despite the erection of snow fences, and travellers are often stranded between 1,000 and almost 1,500 feet above sea-level. Now there are plans afoot to build a motor-way, similar to the Trans-Pennine Motorway being built some distance to the north at the time of writing, over the Woodhead Pass, and much understandable opposition has been provoked by such a suggestion.

This topmost part of the Woodhead Pass is within the Peak District National Park, and it is obvious that the problem of whether economics or the preservation of natural beauty is the most important should not be difficult to solve. The National Parks Act clearly states that in such parks amenity and access are of paramount importance, otherwise there would be little point in designating such areas.

Lieutenant-Colonel Gerald Haythornthwaite, Technical Secretary of the Sheffield and Peak District Branch of the Council for the Preservation of Rural England, has stated in this context that "a six-lane highway cannot be driven over the Woodhead Pass without destroying entirely the remarkable sense of remoteness which pervades the ridges of the Pennine Chain". How right he is, and how ridiculous it would be to destroy that wonderful remoteness for mere material interests!

To the south again, across the wild fastnesses of beautiful Bleak-low, the ancient Roman route, called Doctor's Gate in recent centuries, climbs up the Woodhead Valley and reaches almost 1,700 feet before descending the trench of the Shelf Brook and so to Glossop and Lancastria beyond to the west. The relatively recent Snake road (early nineteenth century), which is the A57 route from Sheffield to Glossop and Manchester, follows partly this Roman route, notably in the upper Woodlands Valley. The moors on both sides of the route have long belonged to the Cavendish family, and the Cavendish coat of arms possesses a snake, hence the name given to this comparatively new road route.

On the southern side of the Kinder Scout massif is the wide and popular Hope Valley. Through this Vale runs the former Midland

Railway route between Sheffield, Chinley and Manchester. Two major barriers prevented this line being built early in the railway era—the high ridge of moorland between Sheffield and the Derbyshire Derwent Valley, and the even higher ridge blocking the western end of the Edale Valley and separating it from the valleys draining to the Goyt trough. Beneath the former ridge the Totley Tunnel was bored, at over 3½ miles the longest underland tunnel in Britain. It runs from west of Totley to Grindleford station in the Derwent Valley. The other ridge was penetrated by the Cowburn Tunnel, a little more than two miles in length. The great castellated wall above the ventilating shaft rising on the heights of Colborne is well known to ramblers, and it is interesting to realize that this shaft is almost 1,000 feet deep.

Men were lowered in an open metal 'skip' after it had been steadied to stop lateral movement. The 'skip' was dropped down the shaft in a free fall until near the bottom, when the winch brake was applied. This free fall was essential to stop the 'skip' setting up a pendulum motion during the descent. John Waterhouse has recalled how his father helped to build Cowburn Tunnel and how the shotfirer was almost left behind down the shaft when one of the men already in the 'skip' caught a boot on its metal sides, the signal to be hauled up after the fuses had been ignited! Cowburn proved a difficult tunnel to construct, and water later collected to a depth of 90 feet in the ventilating shaft. Finally, in 1894, the Hope Valley line was opened to traffic. In the last decade it has often been threatened by the closure of its stations but at the time of writing it is still open to passengers.

There is space to mention only three other routes across the Pennines, and these are again in the Peak District. The first is the old pack-horse route between Chesterfield, Chapel-en-le-Frith and Manchester, an ancient route which was surprisingly direct, considering the physical features involved. Today the eastern section, from Chesterfield by Old Brampton and Curbar Gap, is not followed by a main road, but beyond, up Middleton Dale and over the limestone plateau to Sparrowpit, is the A623, busy with heavy vehicles and cars.

The old route between Buxton and Macclesfield dipped to the

head of the Goyt Valley before climbing to the summit of the moors. The more recent road keeps to the higher ground, at 1,500 feet and more above sea-level. At the summit today stands the well-known Cat and Fiddle Inn, at 1,689 feet above sea-level the second highest public house in England; exceeded only by the equally famous Tan Hill Inn at over 1,700 feet on the winding road over Arkengarthdale Moor—between Swaledale and the valley of the Belah River.

The last route is perhaps the most unusual one crossing the Pennines for it is a combination of water and railway. Sir Richard Arkwright took a leading part in promoting the Act of Parliament of 1789 which put forward the Cromford Canal which would curve up the Derbyshire Derwent Valley as far as Cromford, south of Matlock. Far to the north-west the Peak Forest Canal was completed in 1800, leading up into the Western Pennines from Manchester as far as Whaley Bridge. Between these termini —Cromford and Whaley Bridge—the possibilities of building a waterway were very slender on account of the steep gradients and high altitude attained. Instead a railway route, which joined the two waterways, was planned, built and completed by 1830. It was known as the Cromford and High Peak Railway and opened as a horse-operated line in 1831. Its many inclined planes and tunnels were indeed notable, especially that climbing south-eastwards out of the Goyt Valley and that rising straight up from the Derwent Valley on to Cromford Moor—clearly seen from the A6 road over a mile south of Cromford. Later steam traction was introduced, and stationary steam engines hauled the wagons up the fiercest gradients. The principal of empty wagons being elevated by the descent of heavier laden wagons was also utilized, and another feature was the series of very tight curves on this line, notably above Hopton. Limestone was the major commodity carried, from the many quarries and kilns upon the Carboniferous limestone plateau to the Cromford Canal and, after its abandonment in 1944, to the Manchester-London main line at Highpeak Junction close to the terminus of the canal. Some years before the western end of this unique railway had ceased to function, and now it is completely abandoned; grass grows on those ingenious inclined planes and the stationary steam engines are silent.

Crossing the Pennines is an exciting experience whatever route is taken—over or under. The sounds and feel of a railway tunnel, the lapping blackness of forgotten canal tunnels or the breezy freedom of a Pennine pass; when you have traversed the watershed you have a worthwhile memory. But to cross on foot is by far the most worthwhile and the most memorable.

CHAPTER III

THE FAR NORTH

HADRIAN'S Wall slants up from the east to the north of the South Tyne. It marks even now a boundary between landscapes, a change in character between the Pennines proper (to the south) and the hills which clip gently on by Coldcotes Moor, the North Tyne Valley, up over Thorneyburn Common, The Dodd and wild Burngrange Moor. Imperceptibly the Pennines join the Cheviots, the axis of the watershed changes, and for some distance the rambler following the Pennine Way walks the 'Cheviot Way', the rolling and sheep-shorn crests which gain their highest altitude of 2,676 feet at The Cheviot.

But, for me at least, the northern Pennines lie southwards from Hadrian's ancient boundary, which climbs from the Solway lowlands and eastwards up the narrow valley of the River Irthing and over the northern flank of Haltwhistle Common at over 650 feet above sea-level. Down the eastern flanks of the watershed the remains of the great boundary run roughly parallel with, and high above at some distance, the valley of the South Tyne. About 4½ miles upstream from Hexham the wall crosses the North Tyne and runs directly on for many miles towards Wallsend and the North Sea. The walk along the line of the wall, across the width of England, makes a delightful excursion in either direction, passing the ancient Mile Castles and sites of the numerous forts in their various stages of preservation.

The ridge of the Pennines reaches its highest elevation in this northern area, actually at the gently rounded summit of Cross Fell. At 2,930 feet this is the highest point in England and Wales outside the Lake District and Snowdonia, and in Scotland south of the Highlands. As with so many Pennine heights, Cross Fell's summit is not a dramatically placed spot; it doesn't possess a sharp arête or a dizzy downward view. Cross Fell is not a particularly shapely mountain when viewed from afar either. However, it is massive and crouches hugely on the skyline, often brushed by lowering, dark-shadowed clouds. This height is a climax of all the wonderful eminences of the ridge as it winds up from Peakland, a proper place for the highest point on this widely varied watershed; that is especially so for the hill wanderer exploring from the south towards the north, a gradual progression in height and size.

To stand upon the wilderness atop Cross Fell on a moonlit January night is an unforgettable experience. Deep snow lies frozen to clough and rounded crest, and away into the grey-blue night the wastes sweep out, lost eventually where dark clouds edge the farthest levels. Here is an arctic terrain, an area which many lowlanders would barely believe existed in this country, let alone in England.

Much of Cross Fell and the adjacent hills are composed of Carboniferous limestone, with the well-known Yoredale Beds largely upon the surface, providing the dark and shaley terrain which might, at a glance, be supposed to be gritstone country. Abutting close to this exposed Carboniferous material on the west is a band of more recent new red sandstone, formed of marls and sandstone. Among this west slope confusion are ribbons of volcanic material, the result of instability near the earth's crust long ago. A band of basalts, dolerites and other solidified lavas now lie at the surface in a narrow belt running north-north-west immediately west of Cross Fell's summit. A larger area of this intruded (cooled and solidified beneath the surface) material can be found in Teesdale between Middleton and as far upstream as Unthank, and Greencomb Sike beneath Langdon Common. Other volcanic material immediately west of Cross Fell consists of lavas, tuffs and slates of Ordovician age. The geology of these western slopes is rather complex, though the surface features are relatively simple. In common with other British mountains composed largely of uniform materials—here mainly the Yoredale

Beds overlying limestone—Cross Fell and its neighbours are definitely flat-topped or tabular.

One well-known authority has stated that the three most prominent Pennine hills are Cross Fell, Ingleborough and Kinder Scout. Though these are notable, I would without question add three or four more to the list, some of them more 'prominent' than the last-named of the trio. Cross Fell has weathered relatively evenly to produce a regular form, as with such notable hills as Errigal in Donegal and Suilven in Sutherland. The shape is not so striking, but the mode of sculpture is the same, as is the regular bedding of the rocks.

Stand upon that wilderness top on a wild autumn day and experience the winds which beat in from the west or the north. The build-up in wind speed with a gain in altitude is well known, and recent researches on this particular summit have shown that the average wind velocity was at least twice that prevailing in the neighbouring lowlands, a result which is similar to estimates made in relation to Ben Nevis.

During the night of 14th to 15th January 1968, a wind speed of 134 miles an hour was recorded on the summit of Great Dun Fell (2,780 feet), two miles south-east of Cross Fell, and this represented the highest wind speed ever recorded in England and Wales. Similarly, with regard to cloud cover and humidity; the summits of many of these northern Pennines are covered by low cloud (or shaded from sunshine by higher clouds) for a surprisingly great proportion of the year. Such conditions of high wind speed, high rainfall, a poor sunshine record and low winter temperatures have a startling effect upon the flora of these hills, much of which is virtually sub-arctic tundra, where bog-moss and cotton grass are two of the species best able to withstand the rigours imposed by climate and poor, shallow soils. This was not always the case, however, and F. J. Lewis has recorded the remains of trees from as high as 2,400 feet on Cross Fell. At one time silver birch, pine and some alder, hazel, rowan, scrub oak and willow grew well up these slopes, extending farthest in clough-heads away from prevailing winds. Similar tree-remains have been recorded upon many Pennine hills, and I have often found the

Arkle Beck
(Overleaf) Arkengarthdale from Arkle Town

decaying remains of silver birch on the peaty heights of the Peak District. A change in climatic conditions and overwhelming by peat bogs are largely responsible for the destruction of most of the highland woods. If we could see the Cross Fell of the thirteenth century I am sure that far fewer of those wild slopes would be open and that woodland would extend far up towards the level crest, to thin out at higher levels. From the point of view of climate, flora and fauna, it is true to say that Cross Fell today represents a hill of far greater altitude than it did in the Middle Ages.

The massif which extends southwards from Hartside Height (2,046 feet) to Murton Fell (2,207 feet) and Warcop Fell and includes Cross Fell is really an escarpment presenting a steep, scarp slope to the west, with many swift-running streams like Kirkland Beck and Dale Beck, which feed the River Eden above Kirkoswald. The gentler, eastern dip slopes present rolling moors drained by the headwaters of the South Tyne and the Tees.

There is a fine walking route along the foot of the western scarp slope, from Brampton to Kirkland through the little villages (largely unspoilt) called Croglin, Renwick, Gamblesby and Melmerby. Between Renwick and Gamblesby the lane wanders southwards through the hamlet of Unthank. There are numerous settlements in the Pennines with this unusual name—a hamlet five-and-a-half miles north-west of Penrith; this particular hamlet not far from Cross Fell, nine miles north-east of Penrith; there is a parish not far from Rothbury in Northumberland and another hamlet eleven miles north-west of Barnard Castle in the North Riding of Yorkshire. Far to the south there is an Unthank in Peakland, a lane and an ancient farm above Cordwell Valley in northern Derbyshire. The origin of the name is linked with *unpanc*, the Old English term for 'land held against the will'—a squatter's holding or land claimed and built upon without the consent of the lord of the community or the freeholder. Another suggestion which seems quite as correct as that given above is that the name is an amalgamation of a personal name, 'Hun', and *thwong*, referring to Hun's land measured out with a 'thong of leather'. Maybe the latter is correct; it would seem to be the more

3

Buttertubs pot-hole
(*facing*) *Swaledale sheep on Buttertubs Pass*

acceptable to successive generations of owners of property with this most unusual and ancient title.

When Melmerby is reached, one looks eastwards up the steep, scarp slope of Melmerby Fell (2,331 feet). The line of the Roman Road called Maiden Way crosses the watershed by this scarp slope and down behind the summit of Melmerby Fell towards the north-east and the South Tyne valley *en route* for Hadrian's Wall. From the top of Melmerby Fell in fine weather one looks northwards to the well named Fiend's Fell (2,082 feet) and the Gamblesby Allotments, above the A686 road that climbs between Penrith and Alston, reaching 1,903 feet at Hartside Cross a mile northwards from Fiend's Fell-top. If crossing on this road by car or motorcycle, it is well to realize that at Hartside Cross one is only 143 feet lower than the wild summit of Hartside Height, less than a mile to the north of the road at this pass—though pass is hardly the name for a route which crosses a virtually level summit ridge. In low cloud and/or heavy snowfall this road soon becomes impassable, and it is a long way down to either eastern or western lowlands in such conditions.

Driving eastwards towards Alston on an October day when I had planned to go on to Cross Fell and had been repulsed by low cloud and a gale-force wind, the view southwards from the vicinity of Meathaw Hill was sinister. From the derelict farmhouses beside this road I looked up the blackened head-valleys of the Black Burn to the cloud-shrouded slopes of Cross Fell, five miles away. Deep blue clouds were racing over from the west, and the whole vista was one of melancholy, made all the worse by the swollen, peaty waters of the Black Burn, 400 feet below the road, and the aspect of those empty cottages upon the roadside.

However, the atmosphere changes quickly in the highlands, and, after descending to Alston and climbing the head-valley of the South Tyne high above Garrigill to 1,937 feet at Crookburn Bridge, the sun slanted through the breaking clouds. This head-valley of the South Tyne is strongly reminiscent of the Southern Uplands of Scotland, with scattered coniferous plantations ranging up the hillsides. The similarity is made all the stronger by the presence of Galloway cattle on some of the scattered holdings above Garrigill. The infant Tyne is far below here and branches many times up on to the boggy northern slopes of Tynehead Fell. My road (leading down into Teesdale) turns eastwards for a short distance and then begins the long descent south-eastwards, revealing long views to the distant blue heights of Cross Fell and Dufton Fell on the western horizon. Dozens of white farms dot the valley ahead, like splashes of whitewash or daisies on a lawn. In autumn this upper part of Teesdale is a feast of colour, backed by cloud-dappled, russet moors.

Where the Maize Back joins the infant Tees one is in a wilderness of lonely valleys and high moorland. Just up the Tees from this confluence is famous Cauldron Snout, one of the river's notable falls. Here the peaty water roars down in a cloud of spray over hard rocks, and to many ramblers the river is at its most impressive, more so, some believe, than six miles downstream at High Force. This is England's most famous waterfall and has for a long time been referred to as the country's finest. I came here first on an autumn day of heavy showers, after days of heavy rain, and so the falls were in a relatively impressive mood. The fact that one pays an entrance fee at the road and walks along a well-worn path rather spoils the effect and builds up expectation unreasonably. As one proceeds westwards, the noise of the river increases and, turning a corner amid the overhanging trees, a fine view of the falls can be had. This is perhaps the most impressive point. Upon reaching the close-up viewpoint at the edge of the plunge-pool, where the chocolate water (after heavy rain) swirls, the scale of High Force can be seen to be less than the distant view suggested. I estimate the main fall to be about 45 feet.

After prolonged heavy rain the right-hand branch floods too, and the Tees isolates the bold pillar of rock at the centre of the falls. Normally the best season to see High Force is in late winter, for in autumn the great quantities of peat covering the hills forming the collecting grounds for the Tees absorb much of the rain; only when this great and unseen reservoir is saturated does High Force get most of the rain after it has fallen.

For a more impressive view stand on the rocks above the Force, getting there by means of the higher flight of steps above the most popular viewpoint. The reason for High Force existing at all is quite simple. Hereabouts a sill of molten volcanic material was intruded or forced between beds of rocks already in existence. This sill is of very hard material, has withstood the erosive activity of the ages and is now exposed upon the surface; part of Hadrian's Wall was built upon its eminences and the Tees falls over it at High Force. Associated with it is a remarkable flora, wild plants which find here suitable conditions and ideal mineral salts for their well-being. Many of the plant rarities of the Upper Tees are protected by law, and no one should pick the flowers growing here.

To the south-east is the busy little town of Middleton-in-Teesdale, where the old road from Brough, above the Eden Valley on the western side of the Pennine watershed, comes over and down the Lune Valley. Below Middleton the Tees Valley opens out, and numerous historic and pretty villages are scattered about the valley floor—Romaldkirk with its old church which is worth visiting; Lartington and its park-girt hall; Cotherstone and others. And so to Barnard Castle, with its antiquities and unique site high overlooking the river, almost a Ludlow of the North. There are the ruins of the twelfth-century castle; the imposing ruins of the mill above the Tees; the tall house built in 1483 (now a restaurant) on the steep main street, with three intact and one broken stone figure on their plinths between the first and second floors. The ancient building is whitewashed, and there are four storeys to the bay at the upper end. Then there is the famous Bowes Museum on the eastern edge of the town and the—but one could devote a whole chapter to the attractions of this old settlement which is one of the eastern gateways to the northern Pennines.

A little way downstream from Barnard Castle are the ruins of the twelfth-century Egglestone Abbey, upon the southern bank close to the point where the little Thorsgill Beck joins the river. The late Captain E. Hutchinson of Egglestone Hall used to catch as many as thirty salmon hereabouts in one season, and other anglers recorded catches of thirty-four, twenty-eight and twenty-five. Salmon are nowadays rare in the Upper Tees, thanks largely to the effective barrier put up by pollution from industrial and domestic effluents in the river's lowest reaches. Since the 1920s salmon have been almost completely eliminated from this river because the powerful effluents flowing into the Tees estuary de-oxygenate the water and "make it almost impossible for returning fish to run through in response to the salmon's compulsive urge to reach their spawning beds". Even if a few resolute adults did gain the safe waters above industrial Tees-side, their offspring, those "young smolts heady for the sea and their first migration", often run for the open sea and so perish in the foul estuarine waters before gaining their objective.

Just notice how the metaphorical tide has turned in the last forty years or so. In 1922 there were 5,527 salmon and grilse (young fish returning upstream after one year at sea) taken by nets and 361 salmon taken by rod and line, their total weight being recorded as 59,010 pounds. By 1937 only 23 salmon were sold at Hartlepool by netsmen—and only two rod licences were taken out!

At the present time an attempt is being made to restore the Tees as a salmon river, but pollution is still a very real threat to these superlative fish. Fifty thousand salmon ova have been planted in the upper reaches of the river, but this figure is not so great when we realize the great natural losses to be expected from predation by fish, birds and animals, then attack from predators in the open sea for those smolt which finally get through the terrible barrier of pollution caused by man at the estuary. This must only be considered an experiment, and one not likely to succeed unless man puts a stop to the foul effluents of Tees-side industry.

Of the towns of the northern Pennines two are favourites of mine —Alston and Brampton.

Alston stands on the steep ground rising to the east above the upper valley of the South Tyne. It is surprisingly steep here, and the main street of this lovely little market town is one of the fiercest I have seen. Of course, the place is best known for its claim as the highest market town in England. The 1,000-foot contour crosses that steep main street so that Alston is no more elevated than Buxton, that far larger Peakland spa at the southern end of the Pennines. However, Alston is an unusual little town, with a population of about 2,000 persons, and is more picturesque than Brampton away to the north-west.

For many years I was familiar with photographs of the well-known Market Cross but never had any idea that it was situated in the middle of that cobbled street with a gradient of 1 in 10. The Market Cross, with its timber and tile roof, was originally erected on a site belonging to Greenwich Hospital by the Right Honourable Sir William Stephenson. This man was born at Crosslands in the parish of Alston and elected Lord Mayor of London in 1764. Greenwich and Alston have other links too, for in 1735 the estates of the last Earl of Derwentwater were settled on Greenwich Hospital, and thereafter the church here was closely connected with Greenwich until 1952. The cross was removed from its original site and rebuilt by public subscription in Alston's main street in 1883. What was my shock to see a photograph of this cross in the *Yorkshire Post* of Saturday 8th January 1968, after it had been demolished the day before by a runaway lorry and wrecked beyond repair—all the more sad as the structure was to have been used as the town's symbol on a tourist brochure.

Just across the steep street from the site of the famous Market Cross stands the old Parish Church of St. Augustine. The original building was possibly Saxon, but the earliest definite date in connection with Alston's church is 1154, when King Henry II appointed Galfrid as the Rector of Alston. The building has been rebuilt four times. In 1769 and 1770 it was pulled down and a new church erected by Smeaton, architect of the Eddystone Lighthouse. Just a century later—in 1869—Smeaton's church was demolished and the present one built. It is interesting to examine the stones belonging to former Alston churches now assembled in the south porch, together with the weathervane from Smeaton's church, possessing the date '1770' upon it.

From Alston and its environs one can look out over this north-eastern corner of Cumberland and see the coniferous plantations above Loaning House and Randalholm Hall, and away to a myriad steep, stone-walled fields.

But Brampton is different, a fine little town at 250 feet above sea-level, standing well back from the River Irthing but occupying the lowlands associated with that meandering Cumbrian watercourse. The Roman Wall is about two miles to the north, and so Brampton can be thought of as having been a 'frontier town', a feeling reinforced if one stands upon the motte and bailey dominating the town to the east, where the Normans erected their wooden castle to keep back the Scots. Today the intricate streets and tall, old buildings give the place a decidedly old-world atmosphere. I first arrived there on a cold, wet October evening, when all the hotels were full or closed. As I searched the dim-lit streets, as the rain poured ever heavier down, how I was reminded of corners of Dickens' London. On that first visit there was a strong feeling of a settlement in an inhospitable situation, a lonely, northern land just outside the town. And next morning, as I made towards the south-east, the wild fells were soon seen forming a brown boundary to east and south—Bruthwaite Forest, the Tindale Fells and King's Forest of Geltsdale, rising to the conical 2,039 feet summit of Cold Fell. Aloof fells of the far north, which have more in common with the uplands of northern Scandinavia and Iceland than with the lowlands of southern England.

CHAPTER IV

SWALEDALE COUNTRY

AT SCHOOL I learned the names of the principal rivers running into the Yorkshire Ouse and the Humber by memorizing the composite word *SUNWACDT*—Swale, Ure, Nidd, Wharfe, Aire, Calder, Don and Trent. And the northernmost river is the one which has cut deeply to help in the formation of one of the loveliest of all Pennine troughs. Beautiful and lonely Swaledale; virtually unspoilt by the passage of time, the symbol of all that is joyous when Man and Nature work together in harmony.

The dale at its best is upstream from the village of Reeth, where the Arkle Beck comes down out of Arkengarthdale to the north. The villages which seem to grow from the very dale floor are typically of the Pennines, and some of the most beautiful and unpretentious and unsophisticated settlements left in England are to be found in these recesses, beneath brown and green fell country of infinite charm. There is Healough and Low Row and Gunnerside. There are those three upper-dale villages which come as a surprise to the newcomer descending by the winding moor road from Wensleydale by way of Buttertubs Pass; Muker is the largest, standing close to the confluence of the Muker Beck with the parent Swale underneath Kisdon Hill. This isolated height is something of an island, for the main river flows down to the east of it, while the tributary Muker Beck flows round from west and south, and the road follows this way, up to Thwaite a mile above Muker. My first sight of Thwaite was from that descending hill road over from Wensleydale—suddenly, quite unnoticed previously, there were the brown roofs of close-clustered Thwaite. The place gives the impression of a defensive settlement, not against the violence of Man but more against the violence of Nature on nights of high wind and blizzard conditions, in the same way that an East African village clings together against the great wide 'outside' beyond. At Thwaite, though, there is not much 'outside' but rather 'up' (to the high fells) and 'down' (to the lower reaches of the dale around several corners).

Thwaite is small and unspoilt but can boast of being the birthplace of two world renowned figures. Here were born the eminent naturalists, the Brothers Kearton. Their family had lived hereabouts for generations, and the two boys, Richard (a cripple) and Cherry, attended Muker school. Richard became the famous author of many books, and Cherry became a pioneer natural-history photographer. One of their best books, *With Nature and a Camera*, first published in 1897, written by Richard and illustrated by Cherry, covers a wide variety of natural history and terrain between the south of England and St. Kilda, far out in the Atlantic. The last chapter is entitled "Our Methods of Photography" and gives a real insight into the problems and techniques of natural-history photography in the days when few people showed an intelligent interest in this rewarding pastime—a pastime which the Keartons made a profession. Though they did not remain permanently in Swaledale these brothers always considered it their home and regularly returned to the peace and the haunts of former days, which did not change and have not altered to any marked extent even to this day. Their feeling for Swaledale beneath those hills comes through in the dedication of the above mentioned book to their parents—

> Who now lie sleeping where
> The Rock Thrush pipes his lonesome note
> And the Moorcock becks at dawn of day.

The little road up the dale floor swings northwards beyond Thwaite, through pretty Angram and down to Keld, sheltering under Angram Common and Kisdon Hill and backed by lovely wooded hollows where the young Swale tumbles. Just hereabouts are several fine waterfalls—none large but all worth a visit. They include Kisdon Force, Catrake Force and, above the

village, Wainwath Force. The Pennine Way comes down into
the dale here, through Keld and up over Stonesdale Moor northwards towards Bowes and Teesdale. There is a useful Youth
Hostel here at Keld, overlooking the infant river and not far from
Park Bridge, where one road swings up to the very head of the
valley and over Lamps Moss to Kirkby Stephen, while the other
road climbs up the tributary valley called Stonesdale Moor and
out over very wide, wild country, where nardus grass, rush and
some heather predominate. One could well be in the steppes of
Central Asia; undulating grazing land waving over to far horizons,
and the occasional horse-mounted shepherd on his rounds comes
into view from a distant meander of the Stonesdale Beck. To
some extent this expansive tract crossed by the Pennine Way is
spoilt by the presence here and there of secondhand railway goods
vans placed conveniently for the farmer. No doubt they are most
useful, but it is a pity their presence is necessary, and they are
especially conspicuous on account of the bright colours used to
paint them.

Away to the west are the rarely-rambled hills culminating in
the 2,170-feet-high Nine Standards Rigg, which lies only 3 miles
to the east of Kirkby Stephen. The summit lies in Westmorland,
the boundary between that county and the North Riding of
Yorkshire coming eastwards to within a mile of the road as it
climbs, and the Tan Hill Inn comes suddenly into view to the
north, whitewashed and bleak upon the watershed between the
Swale and the tributaries of the Greta. There are few houses so
wildly situated as this inn, and it can, of course, claim the distinction of being the highest public house in England, standing 1,732
feet above sea-level. Beside the building are the remains of an
older habitation, fallen and grey. This public house is not upon a
main road and has seen better days for hereabouts the Crow Coal
Seam was exploited as early as the thirteenth century and for a
long period afterwards, and the remains of several of these mines
can still be seen upon the 1,700-foot moorland about Tan Hill.
The miners and pack-horse drivers brought good trade to the inn,
but today it relies on the steady passage of ramblers and motorists
upon the Pennine Way. When I was last there a party of three

Leeds ramblers were taking refreshments after the long trudge up from Keld Youth Hostel. They were walking the Pennine Way from south to north in fifteen days and were making for Bowes that night. As we stood upon the moor beside the public house, they disappeared into the long heather which leads down into Frumming Beck. There, carved on the flat gritstone rocks, was the inscription:

> In memory of Susan Peacock, Tan Hill Inn,
> who died 24th May, 1937.
> Lived here since 1902.

From this lonely perch there are wonderful views to the north-west, across to the Cross Fell district of the far north. I was set to comparing this situation with that of the second highest public house in England, the Cat and Fiddle Inn beside the Buxton-Macclesfield road in the southern Pennines. This inn stands at 1,690 feet, and the situation is wild, but not so extensively wild or so remotely situated as here at Tan Hill. There is a rarely accomplished walking route taking in both these high inns, from Tan Hill to the Cat and Fiddle, but it is for the expert and dedicated fell walker and is something of a marathon. More popular is the famous Four Inns Walk, taking in the now-defunct Isle of Skye Inn near Holmfirth, the Snake Inn, the Nag's Head Inn at Edale and the Cat and Fiddle Inn. For some years this route has been walked annually in spring by teams formed from troops of the Scouts Association, and it reached the headlines when lives were lost from exposure on a recent Four Inns Walk as a result of lack of training and stamina.

He who can walk long distances comfortably in the Pennines can with confidence undertake the traversing on foot of terrain in any part of the world.

On a spring day we arrived close to the Tan Hill Inn as the level ceiling of grey and blue clouds miraculously lifted and the sun was able suddenly to light up the moor, gilding the dead rushes and grasses as far as the eye could see. As we looked, a pair of curlews flew quickly overhead against a constant chorus of skylarks, a very different aspect to wild January days when the snow is drifted high under a threatening and heavy sky.

From Tan Hill the road north-westwards takes us in several wild miles into the Eden Valley, while the eastward leading road winds on, slowly loses altitude and comes close above the fast-tumbling Arkle Beck. This is the watercourse of little-known and precious Arkengarthdale. The dale, a tributary of Swaledale, starts life suddenly with forested patches, cultivated fields and scattered farms after the lonely levels of the moor just traversed from Tan Hill and beyond. This side-dale is not so busy as it once was for depopulation has taken place, just as in Swaledale. Besides farming there is little else to occupy the working man, as the lead-mining once carried on in this dale has long since ceased. There were lead-smelting works here too, but these are now in ruins, adding charm in their own way. Upon the heights on all sides there were lead-workings, as on Turf Moor (where local tenants and landowners had permission to cut and cart turf for winter fuel) and on Low Moor above Langthwaite and Booze. Fremington Edge overshadows the Arkle Beck to the north, and up on the far side of the moor called Jingle Pot the lead was extracted at the Hind Rake Vein, open trenching cut deep into the surface. Langthwaite is the main settlement, midway down the dale. The old mill above the road is very picturesque and the view down into the valley is very fine; cottages seem to tumble dalewards, and all about are well-kept farmsteads, while, across the valley, are a few large houses—Scar House, Storthwaite Hall and others—reminding us of the days when there was greater opulence in certain quarters and leisured elegance; qualities often sadly missing now.

Reeth is at the real mouth of Arkengarthdale, a village of about 550 people, set about a village green with the old Black Bull Hotel overlooking all. From the vicinity of Arkle Town the walker can regain upper Swaledale by crossing the spur of high land culminating in the 1,599-feet-high top of Calver Hill on Reeth Low Moor. A track, crossed above Force Gill, crosses Hard Level Gill and climbs and descends to Feetham and Low Row by a straight section of the Swale.

Of all ways into or out of the valley, though, none is better than that which crosses the Buttertubs Pass between Hardrow in Upper Wensleydale and Thwaite. "O'er Buttertubs to Muker a' Keld"—that is a well-known North Riding description of the way over between the two dales. It climbs steeply up out of Wensleydale, winding and unfenced, to reach the 1,726 feet col, where Lovely Seat (2,213 feet) stands only a mile to the south-east, and Great Shunner Fell (2,340 feet) twice that distance to the north-west across particularly ill-drained moorland. The latter hill is wedge-shaped and contrasts with the dark, crouching rock shapes upon the former top. From here the little road plunges directly down into the steep-sided clough of the Cliff Beck; the gradient is far more unrelenting on this Swaledale side. All about is a real panorama of loneliness, and when I was last there a thick cloud cover was tinted grey and gold by a vague sun as we looked northwards. Beyond the hazy depths of the dale ahead were the solid, deep blue outlines of isolated Kisdon Hill (1,636 feet), Melbecks Moor and Arkengarthdale Moor.

At 1,600 feet on the Swaledale side are the two sets of adjoining pot-holes called the Butter Tubs. Centuries of surface drainage water has eroded the limestone into deep holes; semi-circular hollows with walls worn into tiny ridges and hollows adorn the sides of the large holes. Water drains down and disappears into deep fissures; ferns and mosses grow here in profusion in sudden contrast to the bleak moorland vegetation around. It is these pot-holes, which are so aptly named, that give the pass its name.

The dale is almost as well known for the breed of sheep which originated here as for its unspoilt scenic beauty. The Swaledale is today one of the premier mountain and hill breeds, for its hardiness makes it suitable for overwintering on the poorest of unsheltered land, where it can make large areas of otherwise uneconomic moorland an economic proposition. Originally, of course, the breed was found only in the environs of the northern Pennines, especially in and about Swaledale, but nowadays it is a popular sheep for crossing with other breeds which are either slightly smaller in size—like the Scottish Blackface—or are not so hardy. The breed has a shorter fleece at the front than the Blackface so appears rather triangular in spring and early summer before clipping. Its face is dark grey, and its nose is described as "mealy", while its legs are spotted black and grey. In exposed fell country well to the south and west of the Swaledale region a breed even more hardy than the Swaledale is popular; this is the brown-faced and shorter fleeced Rough Fell. Undocked tails are regularly found among the flocks of the northern and central Pennines, as the shepherds believe that an undocked tail offers more protection to the rump in severe weather, and the longer tail is able to swat flies. The poor grazing upon which many Swaledale sheep survive does not lead to excessively loose droppings to foul the rump wool anyway, so there is less likelihood of blowflies laying their eggs here. Swaledale wool is a good protection against snow, while the wool of certain other mountain and hill breeds is better suited to turn heavy rain.

The dale is narrower and more sinuous than Wensleydale to the south, so there is more of the feeling of a true dale here. Looking down the valley one April morning, I watched the sunlight slant in patches upon the interlocking spurs; the dominant feature was the crest of Crackpot Moor—called Blea Barf (1,772 feet)—upon the southern side of the dale. Maybe the scene hasn't altered much in a century, and the stack of freshly riven ash stakes leaning against a dry-stone wall adjoining a brown-walled farm could have been the product of a day's work in any century. But the approach of a flock of Swalesdales down the lane behind me took my attention. The dog was there alright, but the farmer followed in his van, whistling commands to the dog as necessary. Had the farmer been walking, the activity would certainly have looked more picturesque, and more photogenic. Yes, even the dale's-head farmer has had his working life altered; dare I suggest that he is not so generally physically fit as his father or grandfather, who only rode in his gig or trap upon the rough dale lanes between those unchanging hills?

Walking upon the lonely slopes of Angram Common above Keld one can look northwards towards Tan Hill; lonely and lovely moors where the insignificant things of life can be forgotten amid the wonders of great space and bird life of the high tops. We can recall that Tan Hill is virtually as the Keartons knew it, and it was then a left-over from Georgian times. The land-lord in late Victorian times, to quote Richard Kearton, "in spite of being an old man of between seventy and eighty years of age, all spent immured amongst the gloomy solitude of the lonely hills, was as merry as a schoolboy, and laughed at his own jokes until the tears ran down his wrinkled cheeks". Eighteen gallons of ale lasted a month in summer and three months in winter at Tan Hill Inn, and the landlord told the Keartons that eleven consecutive weeks sometimes went by without one stranger entering the place! They were simple, happy folks, and if few are now left with such light hearts at least we may look upon the same unspoilt and happy land under the same cloud-specked sky and listen to the croak of a passing raven or the mew of a gliding kestrel as it quarters these high places.

CHAPTER V

WENSLEYDALE AND WHARFEDALE

THE Yorkshire Dales National Park covers an area of 680 square miles (the third largest National Park in England and Wales), and extends from Langdale Fell (north of Sedbergh near the Westmorland border) in the north-west to Bolton Abbey on the River Wharfe in the south-east. The area includes most of the beautiful dales-country, including remote Dentdale. There are two major rivers draining the region and dozens of lesser ones. These two important ones are the River Ure and the River Wharfe —the former rising at 2,100 feet upon the western flank of Sails (2,185 feet), the highest point of Abbotside Common, running first west, then south and finally turning eastwards near the Moor Cock Inn, five miles from its lonely rising place. For the rest of its journey through the Pennines it trends roughly towards the east in the relatively wide valley called, confusingly, Wensleydale. By Hawes, Bainbridge, Aysgarth and Wensley runs the Ure and then out into ever lower land by Masham, West Tanfield and Ripon. The River Wharfe does not start life with that name, rising as the Green Field Beck at 1,800 feet upon High Green Field Knott and running eastwards through Llangstrothdale before entering Wharfedale as the River Wharfe a short distance upstream from Buckden. The main trend of this river is south-easterly, by Kettlewell, Grassington and Ilkley and leaving the Pennines to run by Otley and Tadcaster before joining the Yorkshire Ouse out on the level monotony of the Plain of York.

But let us look at the upper reaches of these two important rivers in turn, at those stretches most closely connected with the subject of this book.

Hardrow Force, Upper Wensleydale

Below Appersett, where the Widdale Beck comes in from the south-west, Wensleydale is remarkably wide. Looking west along its length in the vicinity of Bainbridge or Ingleby Lodge gives one this impression, with countless groupings of deciduous trees (really copses) ranged along the flat bottom and up the easily sloping sides of the dale. In misty conditions, especially after rain and before the sun has completely dispersed the clouds, this feeling of great scale is strongest. Copses vaguely appear from their mound-top or dale-side resting places, then strengthen in outline and finally stand bold and crisp. After an early morning of heavy, Pennine rain the group of trees upon the round top of a conspicuous hump below Sedbusk did just that, growing into bold outline and looking for all the world like a copse upon the Berkshire Downs; that is until the long, high slopes of Abbotside Common cleared of mist and receded far up into the sky. This confining slope on the northern side of Wensleydale does not create the impression of a dale-side for it is at a comparatively easy angle. Lapwings and larks were calling loudly as we passed a stout, old man leaning against the lane-side wall. He was oblivious of our passing as he took another 'nip' from a small flask taken from his raincoat pocket! The walls of the dale are characteristic, with their three courses of 'throughs' which not only serve a useful function in tying the mortarless joints together but add fascinating decoration to most of the walls in this and adjoining dales.

Another characteristic feature of the Yorkshire dales is the great number of well-preserved outlying barns, usually with a porch and doorway with high, semi-circular arch. This is to allow laden hay-carts to be drawn in out of the sudden rain which so often threatens haymaking in these uplands. A load of hay can then be thrown off into the barn, even though it is raining outside. A last load for the day can likewise be drawn up under the porch with little danger of it getting badly wet during the night. Most of these typical barns, often a good distance from the farmstead, are in a sound state of repair and certainly add charm to the hills and valleys.

Below Aysgarth the dale is reminiscent of parts of the
4

Lower Aysgarth Falls

Cotswolds, and well-wooded by the winding roadside. One may wonder why such a tiny village as Wensley should give its name to so large a valley; the reason is that Wensley was, up to the sixteenth century, a far larger place than it is today. It was the most important market centre for the whole district until the Plague wiped out a high proportion of its people during the sixteenth century, and it never rose to its former status again. Swinithwaite is a particularly attractive village above the river between Wensley and Aysgarth, and close by are the interesting ruins of a medieval Templars' Chapel, shaded above by groves of matured deciduous trees.

Above Aysgarth the chief settlements are Askrigg, (famous for its tradition of clock-makers), Bainbridge (with its green and horn-blower) and bustling, long main-streeted Hawes. Askrigg is my favourite Wensleydale village, with its pleasant, uphill street close by the Parish Church of St. Oswald. Tradition states that the first church was sited in a field on the south side of a stream which runs through the village and near which is a 'cross well', the water from which is reputed to heal sore eyes. The present church was built about 1466, and the round Norman pillars of the north aisle were probably brought from the abbey at Dale Grange. Askrigg was formerly in the parish of Aysgarth, but today the church of St. Oswald is a parish church in its own right. The old coaching house on the left as one goes up the narrow main street is the renowned 'King's Arms', built by John Pratt—a former jockey and Newmarket Trainer—in 1767. The old inn has the atmosphere of former days, with its high-ceilinged public bar decorated with an inverted forest of bacon hooks, and stuffed birds and animals looking out from shaded corners.

I first came to quiet Askrigg on a damp evening when the streets were deserted and immediately took a liking to the place. Its quiet charm so far remains, and 'progress' remains at a comfortable distance. There grew up here in the eighteenth century a close-knit group of clock-makers, whose unique creations went far afield, though I believe that some are still to be found hereabouts. In a charming cottage in the village live those two well-known dales writers, Marie Hartley and Joan Ingleby, who have done so much in recent years to describe their native hills and valleys and the life of the people living there.

The dale has produced its poets, too, and John Thwaite is perhaps the best known. He once so aptly wrote that

> Some lads are fond of gamblin',
> An lots ower fond of ale.
> Ah's fond o t'music milk can mak,
> When it's sylin inti t'pail.

Dairy farming has long been a major agricultural enterprise in Wensleydale. It originated, I suppose, long before the monks of Jervaulx Abbey—far down in pretty, lower Wensleydale—started to produce cheese, using the milk from ewes in their numerous dales flocks. With the growth of dairy farming on the good grasslands above the Ure's banks the tradition of a specialized Wensleydale cheese developed, and today it is known the world over. Few individual farmers produce their own cheese today, but they send their milk to the dairy at Hawes, where large quantities of cheese are made and packed. Many of the farmers supplying this dairy sell the Hawes-made cheeses at their doors, a sort of 'inverted trading' system which works satisfactorily.

The wholesome and upright life of a dales husbandman has for centuries kept the clean farms and fields of Wensleydale (and other Pennine valleys) well filled by farmers and their families. Today the attractions of the 'soft' life (perhaps an appropriate title in one sense) are reducing the density of population, and loneliness fills many of the remoter side-valleys. Take, for instance, that right-bank tributary of the Ure, which flows down from the northern flanks of Buckden Pike (2,302 feet) and is called Walden Beck. It is a narrow side-dale which unluckily looks towards the north and so tends to be a 'late' place in the spring; winter lingers long upon shadowed slopes, indeed, according to many inhabitants, "winter lasts for nine months".

The main settlement is well up this dale, a place of widely scattered farms called Walden. There was once a population of almost seventy but today there are about thirty. The population has halved in the last twenty-five years and, as so often happens, those left tend to be of the older generation. In the mid-dale area of Walden stands Bridge End Farm, the home of Mrs. Jane Thwaites and her son. She is typical of the older breed found throughout the dales and, though an octogenarian living in an old farmhouse equipped with a single gas mantle, she has no regrets and wouldn't wish to live anywhere else. Her memories go back to distant days when the inhabitants of Walden dug peat from the moorland above to provide supplies of winter fuel.

Further up the dale, at the end of the narrow lane winding up from West Burton, stands Kentucky House Farm. It is a four-square farmhouse with a substantial mistal, or shippon, and barn adjoining, sheltered to some extent by tall deciduous trees planted long ago by a sensible landowner. The Wallace family came here in 1946 but didn't intend to stay for more than eight years. These remote dale-heads exercise a strong fascination for those able to live a hard life close to nature and the Wallaces are still there. What could recompense one for the loss of the song of the curlew above the moor or lapwings in spring acrobatics over a nearby meadow? Such a life pays its own dividends, and many remote Pennine dwellings have become less lonely with the arrival of calor gas and electricity and all that that can mean in this technological age.

Of all Wensleydale's charms perhaps the most readily attractive are its numerous falls of water, and two are pre-eminent. There are the Aysgarth Falls, a little below the village of Aysgarth, and Hardrow (or Hardraw) Force, above the little village of Hardrow. At Aysgarth there are really three sets of falls—the Upper Falls by the bridge carrying the lane to Carperby, the Middle Falls under the woods some distance downstream and the Lower Falls down-stream again. The Lower Falls consist of five drops of varying heights or steps, and the sight is one of the prettiest in the Pennines. See them in early morning when the eastern sun is directed towards them frontally, catching every droplet as it dances or races over the several brinks. See them in late afternoon sunlight, when the lighting is behind the cascade and illumines them with subtle, shimmering effect. After heavy rain they are powerful and frightening; after a dry period they are gentle and beautiful; then one can go down the limestone cliffs above the northern bank and walk far out on white, water-worn platforms. From this mid-stream position the eroding effect of the river can be seen to good advantage, having carved and undercut the relatively soluble limestone over many centuries of swirling. There, beneath those short, steep limestone walls, one can see stalactites in the process of formation where chemical deposits are accumulating.

Hardrow Force is a different proposition altogether. It is the highest waterfall in England (except for one or two subterranean ones) and forms a narrow cascade which plunges over a lip of limestone and falls for 96 feet into the edge of a dark plunge pool surrounded on three sides by high, undercut cliffs. Here it is easy to see in cross section a part of the famous Yoredale Beds, the layers of various materials which lie above the Carboniferous limestone proper and below the younger millstone grits. In this area of north Yorkshire the Yoredale Beds reach over 1,000 feet in thickness, and one of the limestones in this strata is called the Hardrow Scar. The gorge, which proclaims the nearness of the fall, has been formed, of course, by the wearing back of the lip by the waters of the Fossdale Gill which plunge over it, and here we can see the successive layers of hard limestones, sandstones and soft shales.

Hardrow village stands upon the Pennine Way and is beautifully situated by the beck, backed by the dark promise—almost a threat—of the tree-bowered gorge where the Force lies hidden. The graceful, high-arched bridge over the Fossdale Gill allows the floodwaters easy passage, and these floods are regular occurrences; in 1899, for instance, a cloudburst on Great Shunner Fell brought down many tons of mud, and the waters washed away the graveyard. Access to the Force is by way of the Green Dragon Inn, where sixpence must be paid for admission. Here are assembled numerous interesting antiquities, and postcards on sale proclaim with the usual degree of exaggeration that "the Cataract is the Highest Unbroken Fall in Great Britain, being a clear drop without dispersion or interception of 100 feet". On entering the gorge, one sees the remains of a stone bandstand, where brass band contests regularly took place in and after 1885 for the ravine has excellent acoustic properties. Likewise choir competitions were held at the top of the Force in Victorian times, but all such romantically-set events have long since ceased. As we continue towards this tall shaft of water, it is easy to realize how the gorge has formed, for above us on the right the soft shales can be seen to have quickly weathered and slipped away, leaving the harder bands of limestone without support so that they eventually collapse.

The plunge pool is known locally as the Dub, and trout are usually present here, unable to make the mighty leap further up-stream! One can walk quite easily behind the Force and look up at the threatening overhangs of limestone. In 1963 the water-fall froze into a solid column of ice and presented a really beautiful sight. Going up the steep, vegetated slopes on the western side of the Force, one can easily ascend through the limestone blocks and gain the exciting top of the fall. I have seen small children jumping across the beck at this point, just above the point where it leaps over the edge. Standing up here gives one some idea, on a smaller scale, of what Malham Cove would have been like in the days when the infant Aire fell over the brink, before it sank into the limestone upstream and so deprived us of an even more specta-cular Force than this one at Hardrow.

In among the limestone clefts and faces here grows a rich and varied flora, and between March and May the outstanding flowering plant is the golden saxifrage (*Chrysosplenium oppositi-folium*), which covers a good area here, its flat, leafy heads of petal-less yellow flowers being unusual in the saxifrage family.

I must confess that the well-known Wharfedale is not one of my favourite Yorkshire dales, and I consider parts of it rather dull. It trends towards the south-east, and, in contrast to the Ure, the Wharfe does not extend up to the headwaters as a beck in its own right. Above Buckden Wharfedale becomes Langstrothdale, and the watercourse is called Green Field Beck, rising at almost 1,800 feet on the western flank of High Green Field Knott (1,959 feet), three miles north of Penyghent's summit. Where Langstrothdale opens out into Wharfedale proper there is a change in direction of flow of the river—from eastward to south-eastward—and the valley opens out as a semi-mature type, with a flat base over which the river meanders, and the whole valley has a U-shaped cross section. Because of these features it is rather monotonous, particularly between Kilnsey and Buckden. The main interest in this section are the pretty settlements nestling along the dale's floor, just above flooding level; settlements like Starbotton and Kettlewell.

On a grey and threatening evening I came this way, over the narrow lane which winds across from Bishopsdale and by the hideous War-Department areas, where one is threatened with shells and bombs for treading the once-unspoilt moorland—may such desecration of God's good land soon be stopped that sheep, man and wild beasts may go again unharmed in this expansive territory. Coming down into Wharfedale beneath Rakes Wood, above Buckden, I was disappointed by the regular lines and apparent monotony of the dale which lay down there before me. The grey weather did not help to charm the parallel-sided dale. The main attraction for me lies in the upper reaches of Wharfedale and its tributaries.

One mile above Kilnsey village the little River Skirface comes down out of lovely Littondale, the main tributary valley of Wharfedale. For much of its length this dale too is U-shaped, with a stream meandering across a flat floor, but it is more varied, and the various woods clinging to the slopes add almost as much charm as do the villages of Hawkswick, Arncliffe and Litton. Romantic Arncliffe, around which Charles Kingsley modelled his *The Water Babies* is unspoilt, and is backed by the high, smooth slopes of the spur called Old Cote Moor, which separates this dale from Wharfedale. Continuing on beyond little Litton, the lane reaches the head of the dale, a wall of fells seems to block further progress, and there, alone under the southern slopes of Horse Head, is the hamlet of ancient farms and cottages called Halton Gill. I first saw this place as a young boy, as we drove up from Wharfedale in the Lanchester 10, and I thought it the loneliest place on earth. There, outside a brown-walled farmhouse, was an old man sitting on a wooden chair, and I have never forgotten the sight. When I returned for the first time recently the place had barely altered. The farms and cottages—one is ivy-covered—cluster, all looking towards the south to gain the most sunlight, and the tiny church with its felled yews has a porch erected in 1914 to the memory of a former incumbent. The biggest house is the Manor Farm, and close by is a very fine example of a dales' barn with typical arched porch built in 1829. Beyond Halton Gill the lane winds on further to Foxup, another lane winding steeply over Penyghent Fell towards Stainforth. Along this partly unfenced lane over the fells one is likely to see part of the well-known Rainscar Dalesbred herd of Galloway cattle, an ideally hardy beef breed for the severe climate and sparse grazing of this district.

The most impressive natural feature of Wharfedale is Kilnsey Crag, close to the village of Kilnsey between Grassington and Kettlewell. The crag, really an outcrop of Great Scar Limestone well in excess of 100 feet high, looks boldly out over the floor of the dale and is close above the road. The top of the cliff overhangs the lower wall and in the section known as the Great Overhang is 45 feet or more out from the base, most of it in the form of a horizontal 'roof'. Joe Brown has described the efforts behind the first ascent of the Great Overhang; how he spent five hours reaching the roof by climbing the smooth wall below it. He has likened the scale of the roof to a "ballroom floor seen in a mirror on the ceiling". With two companions on another occasion he almost reached the end of the difficulties and dropped a piton—it landed 45 feet out from the foot of the face! The first ascent, however, was made by that great cragsman Ron Moseley, after many weeks of difficult progress under the roof. Each weekend he progressed a little further and then descended; at the final effort he spent eleven hours lying horizontally secured to the roof by pitons and rawl-plugs before coming out and up the final wall to the grassy terrace above the crag. Since that time Kilnsey has seen several successful ascents, including a B.B.C. Television film showing the difficulties.

Lower Wharfedale is not, to my mind, truly Pennine and so must not take much space here. The sylvan beauties of this opening-out section are renowned; the Wharfe below Grassington and on by Burnsall and Appletreewick is embowered by trees and softer hills. It is a charming and a pastoral countryside with old halls standing back in small valleys and sheltered by old trees, and if in higher Pennine country I would feel free to use more space in extolling it. Suffice to recall that the woods of Bolton Priory, a few miles upstream from Ilkley, are among the loveliest in Britain. Today the romanticism of the priory, dating from 1151, is retained in large measure, and it is the property of the Duke of Devonshire, whose grouse moors extend high above this part of the dale.

A couple of miles above Bolton Priory, towards Barden, is the notorious Strid—the neck of rocks through which the Wharfe surges and sucks and foams. It is a dramatic sort of place, notably after heavy rain upon the higher fells, but do not be tempted to jump the Strid unless you are skilled and have a life-line held by a team of strong haulers! Many potential crossings have been unsuccessful, and the list of those drowned grows.

Below the arcadia surrounding Bolton Priory the river is overlooked by heather moors above famous Ilkley. Here the Romans built their station called Olicana, and many of the ancient finds of the area are now to be seen in the museum and art gallery housed in the Manor House close to the old parish church. Ilkley can also boast that Wells House—now a College of Education—was the first hydropathic establishment to be built in this country. The most interesting feature of Rombalds Moor is the gritstone outcrop known as the Cow and Calf Rocks, a large boulder adjoined by a lesser one reminiscent of the Sow and Piglet Rocks beneath the Grinah Stones in high Peakland. How strange that a local song has led to this outlying moor becoming world famous. However, these Wharfedale moors are also renowned for grouse, and each autumn the chilly sky echoes with the reports of shotguns fired from turf-and-peat butts. The Duke of Devonshire owns many of these uplands, and the game is strictly preserved.

Gamekeeping is a traditional craft of the Pennines, and before leaving the dale mention must be made of Britain's best known gamekeeper. Walter Flesher lives at Burley-in-Wharfedale, between Ilkley and Otley. For fourteen years Walter took the part of 'Ted Brock' in Children's Hour's "Wandering with Nomad". He is a real gamekeeper, of course, and brought real-life experience and human charm to the microphone—it is a rare thing for an actor to play the part of the man he really is but Walter Flesher did it admirably. Through all those long years I was an enthusiastic listener, and, looking back, that series of programmes did much to foster my innate interest in the countryside. Walter was born in late Victorian times and left school at the age of 12. After work in a woollen mill (where he recalls that his weekly wage was 2s. 3d.), followed by other poorly-paid work, he joined the army in 1914 and was severely injured in 1917, losing his right arm. Up to the outbreak of World War II he struggled along with his own poultry and half-acre of land, becoming a keeper in 1941. Until 1965 that is where Walter remained, giving talks and contributing so much to programmes which included "The Countryside" and "Look". Like so many true countrymen, Walter Flesher knows in depth the land of his birth, and he is contented with the worthwhile, simple things.

CHAPTER VI

IN DENTDALE

OF ALL Pennine dales this is probably my favourite, especially in its upper reaches above Dent Town. Unlike better-known dales, this one opens to the west, drained by the River Dee which rises upon the lonely wastes of Blea Moor Moss. Because of this westward-looking aspect, the dale is missed by many Pennine travellers, and over the years it has been little affected by change, at least upon the surface.

The lane over from the Hawes-Ingleton road (part of the Lancaster-Richmond Military Road) crosses Newby Head Moss at 1,385 feet then soon drops steeply into a fairyland of trees, swift streams and old farms. One of the first features seen is the Dent Head Viaduct carrying the main Midland Region railway line northwards towards Aisgill Summit and Carlisle. This handsome structure took over five years to build, and the locally quarried 'blue' limestone blends beautifully with the surrounding hills. It is at 1,150 feet above sea-level and reaches 100 feet above the beck running in the hollow which it crosses in ten spans. This line does not spoil the tranquil beauty of Dentdale for it simply crosses the very head of the valley and at a considerable elevation, so that it is usually seen only as a distant feature—I would consider it an added attraction in this particular environment, particularly when thundering steam locomotives crossed Dent Fell. Anyway, the line is visible in the dale for less than four miles, between the northern portal of notorious Blea Moor Tunnel and the southern portal of Rise Hill Tunnel.

The River Dee now runs beside the lane, along a flat, shelving bed of rock overhung by trees. Deeside House, formerly a shooting lodge belonging to Lord Bentinck, is a Youth Hostel and is very well situated for exploring this dale and the surrounding sheep-strewn hills. Half a mile below Deeside House we pass the remains of a once-flourishing 'marble' works, and on the other side, eastwards across the mouth of Arten Gill Beck, the second Dentdale viaduct strides northwards. Artengill Viaduct has eleven arches and is 117 feet high, constructed of the once famous 'Dent Marble', quarried locally. The name 'marble' is really a misnomer because it is a fossiliferous, grey-black limestone which can be polished with good effect for decorative purposes. This viaduct presented many difficulties to the builders a century ago, for they had, in places, to excavate to a depth of 55 feet below ground level in order to locate sound rock upon which to build the foundations of the piers.

The walk, or ride, down the dale is always fascinating, and I like it especially on a summer evening when the western light floods up the narrowing confines and spreads brightly on the heights behind. Old farms, ducks beside the beck, goats browsing the hedgerows—and I have never seen more contented lambs in the fields about Cowgill than on an April day of sunshine and white, packed clouds climbing over the fells. Cowgill was formerly known as Kirkthwaite and is the little settlement, albeit scattered, situated where Dentdale turns the corner and looks down towards the west. In the graveyard of Cowgill's small, low church is a memorial to local men killed in the Great War and in World War II. It seems significant that six were killed in the former and only three in the latter; almost certainly this suggests depopulation, a problem especially serious in this loveliest of dales, which I will refer to again presently.

A narrow lane winds steeply up from Cowgill and out on to Widdale Fell. There were numerous coal mines up here and this road was used by miners and their pack-horse trains. Subsequently the Midland Railway Company utilized it and situated their improbable Dent Station close to it at 1,145 feet above sea-level, the highest on any English main line. Though as near to Dent Town as the railway line would permit, it is still four miles distant, and many a bitter remark has been made by local inhabitants.

Typical is the answer to a visitor's question as to why the station was built so far from the village it was meant to serve—" 'Appen they wanted it near t'railway lines."

In severe winter weather, especially when the wind blows snow in from the south-west, this section of the main line high above Dentdale is regularly blocked. Many photographs have been published showing teams of railwaymen digging out marooned trains buried deeply in great drifts of frozen snow.

Well down the dale stands Dent Town, the principle settlement of the dale. It is known as a 'town' but is really only a village; a village almost out of this world in unspoilt charm. If it were in Snowdonia or the Cotswolds it would attract thousands of visitors annually—and thereby lose much of the charm. But here it is, workaday and workmanlike and unpretentious with its lovely, narrow, cobbled street winding improbably between old stone houses and inns. The present population is only one hundred, with approximately 500 in the surrounding district, and slowly the number is falling and the average age of those remaining becoming greater. It is the well-known story of a beautiful old village in a beautiful district which no longer offers sufficient work to its inhabitants. If more work were to be provided in the form of tourist attractions (more hotels, cafés and shops selling senseless souvenirs) the place would quickly lose that very charm which makes it so attractive to the discerning.

Dent Town and Dentdale are the subject of a 'conservation area' recommendation by the National Park (West Riding) Planning Committee at the time of writing, and it may be scheduled soon as a place of architectural and historical interest, which should help to prevent the rape of the present unself-conscious atmosphere. However, there is already among local inhabitants a considerable amount of resentment of the way in which dale's cottages and farmhouses are being bought or tenanted by townsfolk to be used as 'retreats'. In this way a growing proportion of habitations are empty for most of the year, and local shopkeepers are steadily losing an increasing amount of trade. What will the outcome be for this quiet Pennine corner? It must be either greater depopulation and peace or increasing intrusion by visitors, with the inevitable destruction of the very atmosphere which attracts them.

Dentdale has produced several notable sons. The great block of Shap granite in the main street of Dent Town is a memorial to Adam Sedgwick, who was born here in 1785, when his father was the vicar and schoolmaster. Adam became a Canon of Norwich Cathedral and a senior Fellow of Trinity College, Cambridge. For fifty years he was the Woodwardian Professor of Geology. It is to him that we owe the name given to the surface limestone in this part of the Pennines—Great Scar limestone—which has stuck down to the present time. High up on the inside of the south wall of the parish church there is a memorial tablet to this illustrious Dentman which includes the following words:

> As a man of Science and a Christian
> he loved to dwell on the eternal power
> and godhead of the Creator, as revealed
> in Nature.

His researches in the field of geology led him to appreciate in ever greater measure the great power and wisdom of God, not (as so often today) to have his faith lessened and brought to an unsatisfactory nought.

The parish church of St. Andrew was founded about 1080 and may have come into the care of the monks of Coverham Abbey. It was rebuilt in 1417 and restored in the sixteenth, eighteenth and nineteenth centuries. It is a large church for such a small settlement, and this underlines the fact that the population of the area was once much greater in the days of the knitting industry, when most of the local inhabitants carried on this traditional industry in their homes. The wool from local sheep was used, and Dent knitwear was famous over a large part of the north.

A particularly attractive feature of the tower is the clock face, painted dark blue with the fingers and divisions of time picked out in gold, as is the date, '1828', when the clock was installed. In the tower are six bells, and since 1953 they have been rung with apparatus operated by the sexton single-handed. On a sunny evening this old man took us into the base of the tower and gladly showed us the apparatus. He suggested that my friend climb the narrow, wooden stairs to the bell-loft, and then, with a wicked smile, he volunteered to show me how the bells were rung. My friend quickly descended—not a little deafened!

"Won't the people of Dent wonder why you are ringing the bells at this unusual time?" I asked.

"Oh, no! They'll all be pleased to 'ear 'em ringin'," was his reply; and that somehow typified the happy, unsophisticated charm of Dent Town and its dale. Country people in rural areas aren't, of course, governed by rules of that sort, about when the bells should or should not be rung.

Miles Mason (1752–1822) was born here. He was the founder of the famous Ironstone Pottery, and his three sons, William, George and Charles, improved and patented it. The original designs of these men are still being produced near the original pottery, at Lane Delph in Staffordshire. Towards the end of his life Miles Mason returned to his native dale and lived at Whernside Manor, a Georgian mansion set among trees near the mouth of Deepdale, a couple of miles up the dale from Dent Town. Today this place is owned and used by the Scouts Association, and parties come here to learn about and enjoy the countryside and the wild fells around.

From the summit of Whernside (2,419 feet) in clear weather one gets a very good general impression of the dale. There is a mass of many greens and some browns, broken up by the darker boundaries of walls and hedges. Here and there a knot of shadow suggests an outlying farm, and the trenches formed by the becks draining southwards off Kirk Bank and Hall Bank are picked out in deeper shade, while, up and beyond, the open moor rising to Aye Gill Pike (1,825 feet) gives the onlooker a real sense of space and of freedom. Yes, Dentdale (with its enclosing fells) is a gem which the wanderer on foot should not miss. How long it will remain in such a condition is not certain, for the greed of some men is not to be reckoned with.

CHAPTER VII

WHERE BLACK MEETS WHITE

TOGETHER with the Peak District the area of the central Pennines known as Craven is the best known and most widely visited in the whole of the Pennines. It has a charm all its own, a charm largely the result of the Great Scar limestone which occupies much of the surface of the district. The actual district can be thought of as extending from Ribblehead in the north-west to Long Preston in the south-west and from Great Whernside in the north-east to Barden Fell (above Appletreewick) in the south-east. In other words, the valleys of the upper Ribble, the head of the Aire and the Wharfe well down into central Wharfedale, and the uplands between and on either margin.

A glance at a geological map of the Craven district shows that the area is not entirely surfaced by the Great Scar limestone. All around the younger beds of millstone grit cover the higher hills and there remain scattered areas of Yoredale Beds—sandstones and soft shales—and Bowland shales on the surface, to add to the complexity and a greater variety of scenery. But Craven is a text-book countryside for the student of geology and physical geography, and of field studies in general. To the district every year come parties without number to look at the origins and present structure of the Pennines.

Across the breadth of Craven run three faults or weaknesses in the surface rocks which have resulted in vertical displacement of rock masses so that sudden changes of rock type occur hereabouts. Near Stainforth, for instance, we can walk northwards up the floor of the Ribble Valley from Great Scar limestone and on to much older rocks, including the granites quarried in the district

64

Ingleborough and limestone pavement

west of Horton. This is the line of the North Craven Fault which crosses the district from Austwick and Stainforth to Burnsall. The Mid-Craven Fault extends from Settle in the west to Linton and Burnsall, while the South Craven Fault trends from Austwick and Giggleswick Scar south-eastwards to the upper valley of the River Aire. This sounds all very complicated but when seen on a geological map looks quite simple. Immediately to the south of the Mid-Craven Fault is a series of prominent hills of reef-limestone, which include High Hill, near Settle, and the trinity of conspicuous heights south of Malham called Burns Hill, Cawden and Wedber. These were once 'flat reefs' between a warm sea in Carboniferous times, composed of calcite-mudstones without many (if any) fossil remains. These are very similar in form and origin to the reefs which occur in south-western Peakland and include the spectacular conical hills of Chrome and Parkhouse.

Craven is especially notable for its high, isolated hills, its deep and various pot-holes, the limestone pavements and their associated wealth of flora. The great trinity of Whernside, Ingleborough and Penyghent are the subject of a separate chapter so suffice here to say that they are notable Craven hills, almost peaks, with more character as individuals than the majority of Pennine hills. All three are built of Great Scar limestone upon which rest the successive bands of Yoredale Beds and, as a protective capping upon each, the resistant layer of millstone grit which preserves their special shapes in the face of the passage of aeons. But there are other fine summits in this district, including Great Whernside (2,310 feet) at the head of Nidderdale, Buckden Pike (2,302 feet) above upper Wharfedale, and that great mass backing the Malham district and culminating in the millstone grit capping upon Fountains Fell (2,191 feet). The top of this big hill is undulating and not the best place to be when damp mist settles, and in such conditions the two 'stone men' nearby take on the appearance of supernatural shepherds. Up here are the remains of ancient mines, where long ago the coal measures trapped here were exploited, but now the shafts have been rendered harmless to the wanderer as they have, unlike similar shafts on Tan Hill, been filled up. There is an old stone building standing still, a memorial

5

Penyghent from Horton-in-Ribblesdale

to the endeavours of miners of past centuries. The Pennine Way crosses Fountains Fell by way of Tennant Gill in the south-east and down to Rainscar House Farm on the Stainforth-Halton Gill lane to the north of the hill. Fountains Fell was once the property of the Cistercian Order based upon Fountains Abbey, near Ripon. It was one of the largest Cistercian establishments in England, having been erected between 1132 and 1147, and it was the members of this order who not only established scientific methods of farming in the Middle Ages but also founded the woollen industry based upon their large flocks. The wool from their hill flocks upon Fountains Fell would be important and helped to establish the woollen trade in the West Riding of later times.

The great holes eroded in the Great Scar limestone of Craven by centuries of surface drainage are too numerous to describe in detail here. One could spend a lifetime visiting and exploring the best examples of these pot-holes and it was these 'subterranean mountain-sides' which first appealed to me, in those days of hidden hill-secrets, full of enigma and promise of true romance. Hunt Pot, for instance, is a frightening place, lying upon the open, western flanks of Penyghent at about 1,300 feet. It is a long narrow opening, only 6 feet wide but 200 feet deep. A little stream is cruelly swallowed by the pot and re-emerges at Douk Ghyll Scar a little way above Horton-in-Ribblesdale. Half a mile north of Hunt Pot is a different sort of swallow-hole altogether in the form of Hull Pot. Here the Hull Pot Beck leaves the Yoredale Beds and reaches limestone, where it has eroded a great opening 300 feet long and 60 feet wide. Its depth is 60 feet, and water percolates away through the rock and emerges at Brants Ghyll Head, north of Horton village. After heavy rain the whole pot-hole has been known to fill up, but normally the stream soaks into 'the great sink' before reaching the brink. The waterfall is only present when rain has fallen on the heights over a long period. Both re-emergences mentioned here are at points where the limestone ends to reveal the old and impervious pre-Carboniferous rocks upon which Horton stands. Rowten Pot, near Whernside, is 365 feet deep, but of all British pot-holes the most famous is Gaping Ghyll to the south-east of Ingleborough. Here the streams draining

Clapham Bents and Simon Fell fall 365 feet vertically to the Great Chamber, where the chill moor water fans into a crystal display. The magnificent vault would really contain a complete cathedral and is awesome in the extreme. The first explorers found the skeleton of a fallen shepherd at the foot of the main shaft, but since those far-off days most of the extensive cave system has been mapped and revealed as a system with over three miles of passages and various entrances to the outside world. One of these is Bar Pot Aven. Hensler's Passage consists of a tunnel nearly 1,500 feet long and with a maximum height of 18 inches! To enter by the Bar Pot Aven system and approach the Great Chamber from, as it were, one side is suddenly to realize great space and the grace of falling water and the beauty of light on thousands of droplets caught in the distant, descending sunlight. From time to time a caving club erects a bosun's chair and winch at the mouth of Gaping Ghyll, and the visitor can be lowered into the Great Chamber and see the magic world of the chemical action of rocks and water over great periods of time—stalactites and stalagmites and crystal formations.

Then there is Hellan Pot, the Calf Holes, Ingleborough Cave above Clapham where one is conducted round the underground world, there is Alum Pot and—but I could continue to list and describe underground Craven for a long time and space would not allow it. Suffice to say that the area offers as much to the speleologist as to the rambler and the naturalist.

The road up Ribblesdale from Gisburn to Settle is a favourite of mine as main roads go for it has trees, high walls and old houses; it also has forward views as one goes northwards of the hills to come.

Settle is the major settlement of Craven. It received its first market charter from Henry Percy in 1248 and was originally in the ancient parish of Giggleswick so that Settle's parish church is comparatively modern—1838—but its particular interest is that it contains a memorial plaque in marble to the men lost during the construction of the 72 miles of the Settle-Carlisle railway (1869–1876), which cost the Midland Railway Company almost £3½ million. Another plaque to the lost railway constructors is to be

found on the inside of the west wall of the little church at Chapel
le Dale in the valley of the River Greta. Settle clings somewhat to
the steep limestone country and faces westwards over the Ribble
valley. A steep lane climbs up onto the limestone country leading
to Malham. At Fern Cottage, close to the market place, lives the
well-known portrait artist Harold Lisle. He came to Craven from
London some years ago and continues to paint and sketch in pain-
staking detail. On the walls of Fern Cottage are hung some of his
remarkable portraits—one shows his grandfather in old age and
was sketched when the artist was only 12-years-old. Another of
his sleeping sister was completed when he was 16.

Less than a mile to the north-west lies Giggleswick, across the
floor of Ribblesdale. Here flows the little River Tems, which rises
at a notable Ebbing and Flowing Well under the limestone of
Giggleswick Scar. It is active after heavy rain, is caused by the
action of a double siphon far below ground and was remarked
upon by a writer in 1612 as being a noteworthy sight of the
district. The old church of Giggleswick is dedicated in honour of a
Christian princess, St. Alkelda, and stands not far from the public
school in the village. The school is, of course, one of the most
notable in England and received its royal charter in 1553. During
Victorian times there was a substantial growth, and this has been
maintained ever since. These days boys of the school regularly
undertake the Three Peaks route (the subject of the next chapter)
on foot, and the well-sited situation of Giggleswick in relation to
so many interesting features of the mid-Pennines has fostered here
a great feeling for wild places, above and below ground. Some
confusion exists over the site of an observatory at the school. Seen
from road or railway in the vicinity of Settle there appears to be
such a building, but this is the copper dome of the school chapel,
built to commemorate Queen Victoria's Diamond Jubilee at a
cost of £30,000. To complicate matters, it is true, however, that
during a total eclipse of the sun in 1927 the Astronomer Royal
and his staff positioned themselves on a hillock beside the Chapel.

Extending to the north-west above the village is the famous
limestone scarp of Giggleswick Scar, a precipice of the Great Scar
limestone outcropping as a result of a lengthy fault-line, part of

the South Craven Fault. The limestone suddenly overlooks mill-stone grit and, just as suddenly, the natural vegetation and the scenery in general alters character. Natural deciduous woodland covers much of the lower slopes and hides a large proportion of the scar when seen from the main road which ascends from Settle towards Kirby Lonsdale just beneath the scarp face. The top of the scar attains over 900 feet above sea-level and leads northwards towards waterless country so typical of limestone Craven, where pre-historic man erected burial mounds to the perpetual memory of the dead.

Giggleswick Scar is a very good and impressive example of exposed Carboniferous limestone at a fault-line, but two other places in the district are classical in the true meaning of the term; two places where limestone rises above the ordinary to become grandiose, each in its own peculiar way. First, then, comes Gordale Scar, $1\frac{1}{2}$ miles to the north-east of Malham village. There exists a particularly impressive aerial photograph by C. H. Wood show-ing the full extent of Gordale—its scar and its gorge. One crosses the flat pasture fields from Gordale Bridge and soon the narrow confines at the mouth of the gorge are entered. High up on both sides, where the white rock is exposed and partially eroded into scree, are yews and various species of deciduous trees. Suddenly Gordale asserts itself—and that is one reason why I prefer it to Malham Cove—as one turns to the right; there above are two falls where the Gordale Beck plunges from the level of the upper gorge. After heavy rain the place is filled with the noise of falling water, reverberating from cliff to cliff. One cannot fail to be impressed by this piece of the Pennines in such conditions, and it is easy to see why Victorian travellers came here and why many went away feeling that they had "intruded upon the inmost thoughts, the utter heart of Nature". Many notable artists have painted the classical view of the twin falls, with the natural limestone arch above the higher one, where the beck has eroded its way through a narrow wall of rock. In a vague sort of way the place has the atmosphere of Devil's Bridge in mid-Wales though, of course, the bridges there are man-made and the gorge more densely vege-tated. One can quite easily scramble up the left-hand side of the falls and walk out onto the narrow promontory of limestone and thence over the bridge and so get a fine downward view of the lower gorge and the sides of the scar. But behind is the portion—and a far larger portion—of the gorge which is not so well known or visited. That brings us back to the aerial photograph by C. H. Wood, for it shows the full extent of the gorge as it recedes away across cloud-shadowed Malham Lings for a mile and a half northwards. Upstream again, the beck drains a pocket of marshy territory immediately to the east of Malham Tarn and actually starts life at almost 1,500 feet upon the limestone of Great Close. The presence of an area of impervious pre-Carboniferous rock to the north of the North Craven Fault has caused both Malham Tarn and the marshy ground just mentioned to form, prevented from draining away through the porous limestone as they otherwise would.

A fine circuit for an afternoon is to go up to Gordale Scar from Malham village, ascend the gorge above the scar and, on reaching the marshy ground under Great Close Scar, turn to the west and so around the shore of Malham Tarn. It is a remarkable little lake and one of the very few natural ones in the entire length of the Pennines. Standing at 1,228 feet above sea-level, the woods on the northern bank help to shelter Malham Tarn House from the weather. This building is now owned by the National Trust and leased by the Field Studies Council as a field studies centre, where parties come to stay and discover some of the intricacies of this varied limestone country. Many people consider the stream feeding Malham Tarn and draining it at its southern corner is the young Aire, which later sends its soft water down through the woollen towns of the West Riding, but it is really only a tributary of that river. A little distance below the outflow from the Tarn the stream is soaked up into the porous surface rock and re-emerges at Aire Head Springs some little distance below Malham village—not at the foot of Malham Cove, another popular misconception.

Malham Cove is one of the great show places of the Pennines and has an entirely different atmosphere from Gordale Scar. The stream draining Malham Tarn once flowed down the now-dry valley above the cove and so over the great lip and down the great face as a wall of water considerably higher than the Niagara Falls. Today the cove is quiet, and a clear beck—the Malham Beck—emerges from the foot of the cliff after a subterranean journey of over 1½ miles from above New Laithe. My first sight of Malham Cove was on a grey and misty day, when the great wall of limestone came and went in the poor visibility and much of its impact was lost. On a subsequent visit the spring sunshine lit up every terrace and vertical crack in the face, and the deciduous trees crouching below and upon the cove were beginning to burst their leaf buds. On the grassy slopes at either side, which give easy access to the top of the cliff, celandines, dog violets and buttercups were in full bloom. Hartstongue fern grew up from the great cracks in the pavement of limestone on top, and jackdaws were busily engaged in family affairs as we looked down from the rickety rim. On that occasion, I recall, 7-years old Roy Clarkson of Rawtenstall, in Lancashire, was ascending a terylene rope aided by metal clamps and nylon stirrups right up the centre of the cove. As he ascended he slowly revolved, for the rope hung out from the face, until he reached the lip just beneath the top. He was able to count the assemblage of rawlplugs inserted by members of the La Ragni Club when Robin Strange and Trevor Briggs made the first ascent of the directissima route. The climb took four or five days and involved the use of alloy self-drilling anchors of 3,000 pounds breaking strain. It has been stated that the route should be sound for up to twenty years before the bolts would need renewing.

After little Roy had been helped over the lip by his father, he was lowered, like a spider at the end of its silken line, to the bubbling mouth of the beck. Because he was only a little lad his presence upon the face of Malham Cove exaggerated the scale of the place by at least twice, as one tended to regard him as full-size in such a spectacular situation.

Because Craven possesses so many first-rate features of the Pennines—Penyghent, Gaping Ghyll, Gordale Scar and Malham Cove—it has become over-popular. Malham village is spoilt by the natural tendency to cater for the needs of visitors. At holiday times crowds enter the place, and the hotels and cafés are packed with people. Even pot-holes now have their own peculiar problems, and there has recently been legitimate criticism of some types of pot-holes by members of Settle Rural Council. Six bags of litter were cleared out of Bar Pot, below Ingleborough, after the Easter holiday of 1968. The problem of contamination of local water supplies is a real one, especially when one recalls that six bodies were buried in the Mossdale Cavern above Grassington in 1967. There have been suggestions that popular pot-holes should have locked entrances so that only experienced and responsible clubs and individuals could gain access, but the Medical Officer of Health for the area has stated that "the responsibility of letting people down these pot-holes rests with the owners concerned". May commonsense rise to the occasion and those who intend to spend a long period underground at one time realize that they might well be endangering the health of local inhabitants and their animals by so doing.

Though Craven is bedecked with many fine cavernous systems, the heights of the lapwing and the curlew are its crown.

CHAPTER VIII

THE THREE PEAKS

THE trio of Craven heights which have come to be known throughout the world of British mountaineering as the Three Peaks rise in comparative isolation from the general level of the limestone surface about the upper reaches of Ribblesdale. They form a right-angled triangle with a summit at each angle—Whernside (at 2,419 feet, the highest) in the north, Ingleborough (2,373 feet) at the right-angle and Penyghent (2,273 feet) in the east.

For thousands of years these peaks—their shape rather than their altitude defines them as mountains in their own right and worthy of this title—have risen in singular grandeur above the dales and plateaux of this part of western Craven. Of all Pennine tops, surely Penyghent is the most shapely and comes close to Suilven and Tryfan in possessing, in certain lighting conditions and from certain directions, a spectacular profile relatively rare in British mountain architecture. I can remember my first sight of it as a child, from the lane winding over from Halton Gill to Stainforth. It was one of the first dramatic hill-shapes of my experience and helped to instil a deep affection for high places. Penyghent has often been likened in profile to a maned lion and there are similarities, but comparison with a great ship at sea seems more appropriate, notably from the classic vantage points of Dale Head above Stainforth and from near Horton-in-Ribblesdale.

At any rate the most fascinating parts of the mountain are the western and southern flanks, for here the three dominant surface rocks of the district are exposed in quite dramatic form. Looking from either Dale Head or Horton-in-Ribblesdale, the southern end of Penyghent is seen to rise in two steep steps with more gradual slopes between, and from close under these steps—at Gable Rigg—the succeeding strata is readily visible. The foundations are of Great Scar limestone, and there upon this great outcrop, notably on the western flank a little way below the 2,000 feet contour, a variety of interesting flora is found. The queen of these varied mountain plants is purple saxifrage (*Saxifraga oppositifolia*), and if one comes here in April the name Penyghent will forever afterwards be connected with that beautiful alpine. The easily-inclined terrace on top of the limestone is well littered by fallen shales of the Yoredale Beds above and by blocks of millstone grit which have tumbled from the summit capping of that rock. The change from limestone to Yoredale Beds and gritstone is very abrupt, and in a matter of yards the rambler on Penyghent's south ridge will see the transition completed. The most obvious change is the steep wall which climbs the ridge on one's left-hand —suddenly it changes from grey to brown, limestone to grit.

Viewed from Dale Head Farm and its famous and regularly photographed limestone pavement at 1,390 feet above sea-level, the mountain looks remarkably close, and it is not a long walk over boggy ground by Churn Milk Hole (a collapsed swallowhole) to Gable Rigg. I well remember a sultry spring evening when there was thunder about and the songs of larks and lapwings mingled with lamb's bleatings. By the time Gable Rigg had been gained, grey and blue mists were swirling over Fountains Fell and over the Forest of Bowland far over to the south-west. The thunder rolled closer as the storm moved up out of Lancashire, and as there was only an hour of daylight left I descended, thinking this course the most discreet. The storm never came, though there were cloud-bursts in the Forest of Bowland and at Ingleton not far away to the west.

Next morning I reached the summit in fine conditions in three-quarters of an hour from the road near Dale Head; an hour is a comfortable time to reach the top from here, the distance being about two miles. From the graceful cairn and triangulation station on the summit ridge there are attractive views on every side—Ingleborough is six miles to the west and does not look so large as from other angles. Whernside looks deceptively insignificant, 7½ miles to the north-west beyond the grey block of Ribblehead Viaduct. Away to the north the bold escarpment of Wild Boar Fell (2,324 feet) can be made out high above Mallerstang Common at the Head of the Eden Valley. In certain lighting conditions the pool of water at the important limeworks beyond Horton-in-Ribblesdale takes on the colour of eau-de-nil, a great contrast to the subtle colourings of these Pennine slopes and caused by the sunlight being reflected in the water in which are suspended innumerable particles of lime. Care must be taken in bad weather to avoid the steep gritstone crags which bound the western slopes under the summit. The rock is not very sound, and, though numerous routes have been climbed here, the material does not compare with the millstone grit found in the Peak District or near Almscliffe in the West Riding.

Ingleborough is exactly 100 feet higher than Penyghent and is a more popular summit, for it lies closer to such well-visited villages as Clapham and Ingleton. From the nearest road, however, it entails a longer and generally steeper climb than does Penyghent. The quickest way to my knowledge is from the environs of Chapel le Dale in the valley of the River Greta, where the Lancaster-Richmond Military Road climbs towards Ribblehead and so on to Hawes.

Extending as a terrace or ledge above the Greta Valley is a block of exposed Great Scar limestone, seen on the Ordnance Survey map as an area where the surface streams draining Ingleborough's northern flanks disappear. The water re-emerges near the bottom of the valley. On top of the terrace one sees a spectacular table of weathered limestone, white slabs rounded into ridges and deep, dark grooves—the well-known 'clints' and 'grykes' of physical geography textbooks. The former are the upstanding pinnacles and the latter the dark clefts between, largely produced by solution along joint planes by acid rainfall. The 'grykes' contain a wealth of characteristic flora, notably hartstongue fern (*Phyllitis scolopendrium*) and herb robert (*Geranium robertianum*). Here one can walk a considerable distance upon the interesting pavement, and at its northern end, below Gauber High

Pasture, is a plantation of mixed trees, clinging to the porous rock in all manner of shapes. There are conifers and deciduous broad-leaved trees here, not far above the Lancaster-Richmond Military Road. Out on the open, bleached pavement it is all very reminiscent of the wonderful Burren country of County Clare in western Ireland, almost a stony desert at the edge of water-logged mountain pasture upon the adjoining Yoredale Beds.

Ahead of us here the great and shapely bulk of Ingleborough rises, the great thickness of Yoredale Beds obvious, and the thinner capping of millstone grit above it conspicuous again. Upon this level area, where black meets white, is the large swallow-hole known as the Braithwaite Wife Hole; somewhat disappointing when examined for the base of the great 'swallow' area has no obvious hole as at Gaping Ghyll or Hunt Pot. More rewarding and even terrifying is the Stygian chasm some distance nearer Ingleborough, where the surface stream falls into a sub-terranean canal walled by black cliffs. The water is not too far below the surface, and the splashing of the descending water is loud. This particular chasm extends for some distance and is roughly fenced around in an attempt to prevent sheep and cattle from straying too near.

From here it is possible to strike straight up the steep, scarred north face of the mountain and that is the quickest—and my favourite—route to the broad summit. There is an intermediate ledge or shelf a little way below the top, where the capping of millstone grit begins. This is the route usually taken by the Three Peaks runners which will be referred to later. The top is a surprise, a veritable table-top which is prevented from rapid erosion by the hard grit. In sunlight in spring the table-top is laid with orange, the dead molinia grass of last season. There are two great cairns of stone, a triangulation station and a useful, four-walled windbreak incorporating a viewer.

Other viewpoints known to me have an informative viewer, like the ones upon the summit of Lose Hill in Peakland and on the Worcestershire Beacon in the Malvern Hills, but this is more elaborate and can be extremely valuable in bad weather, as one is sure to find one side of it sheltered from the wind. It was erected

by the Ingleton Fell Rescue Team to commemorate the Corona-
tion of Queen Elizabeth II in 1953, and the brass plate on top
indicates most of the interesting features which are visible in clear
conditions, together with the various distances involved. Examples
of this extensive viewpoint are:

Pendle Hill, 22 miles to the south.

Morecambe, 30 miles to the west.

Barrow-in-Furness, 35 miles to the west.

Snaefell, Isle of Man, 84 miles to the west-north-west.

Scaefell Pike, 39 miles to the north-west.

Up here, on this table-top, the world seems almost out of
reach over the brink on every side, and it is little wonder that pre-
historic men chose Ingleborough's summit as a defensive site. The
flora and fauna of the area has been described in copious detail,
and there is insufficient space to say more than a passing word
here; both Penny and Gerarde remarked upon the typically
Pennine cloudberry (*Rubus chamaemorus*) in the sixteenth century
as growing profusely "on Mount Ingleborrow the highest in all
England". Though their topographical accuracy left something to
be desired, their botanical observation was accurate.

Going up the hill from Chapel le Dale I take about one and a
quarter hours, the quarter of an hour being taken to climb the
steep slope to the summit (the north-west face) over Yoredale
Beds and millstone grit. From the top one looks northwards to
the great, grey mass of Ribblehead Viaduct and straight on up
the railway lines to the romantic southern portal of Blea Moor
Tunnel. Immediately to the left rise the slopes of Whernside—
not, of course, to be confused with the lower Great Whernside
between Wharfedale and Nidderdale over to the east. Whernside
is the senior member of this venerable trinity, the highest by 46
feet and the least impressive in form to most people. It is a long,
rolling ridge which rears up northwards between Kingsdale and
the Greta Valley and, beyond the summit, slips steeply down to
overlook Deepdale and Dentdale. One of the popular routes up
Whernside is from Ribblehead, beneath the arches of the viaduct
and so by Winterscales Farm. Here the farming pattern has
changed little in the last half-century, and the farmers still inspect

their sheep on horseback. It is a rewarding sight to see a distant shepherd on horseback on the flanks of Whernside at lambing time, reminiscent of the practices of Lakeland and Southern Uplands sheep farmers, and is becoming rare outside the heights.

From Winterscales it is best to make straight up the south-eastern flank, avoiding the ill-drained grazings above the farm. Another way is to follow the railway lines to the southern portal of Blea Moor Tunnel and then cut up to the top—this way takes me fifty-five minutes and a good bit less the direct way from Winterscales. From the summit, obviously a ridge and more so than Ingleborough and Penyghent, there is a particularly good view into parts of Dentdale. The two viaducts and the railway line at the head of that dale are conspicuous, as are the greens of lower Dentdale, backed by Rise Hill and that in turn backed by the great bulk of Bough Fell (2,216 feet). Distantly, like the last hill on earth, the escarpment profile of Wild Boar Fell peers over these intermediate heights and effectively adds to the sense of space so often apparent in the highest Pennines. Away to the north-west are the crumpled crests of the Lake District hills, with the shapely Howgill Fells nearer. In sharp contrast we can look over blue space to the freshness of Morecambe Bay and the coast of Furness in the west.

One of the height's most interesting features is Whernside Tarns, a group of small lakes or pools on the northern flank. Black-headed gulls nest here, and in spring and early summer one is able to watch flocks of these sea birds as they search for food and squabble over territorial rights at the breeding ground, an unexpected contrast to the curlew and golden plover and skylark which are the usual inhabitants of the area at this altitude.

It is only to be expected that three such equal and interesting hills lying in close proximity to each other should attract the attention of ramblers—not simply as individual hills but as a group, an entity which has come to be known as the Three Peaks. When D. R. Smith and J. R. Wynne-Edwards walked over all three hills in July 1887 a tradition began which is more popular than ever today. After their day's teaching at Giggleswick School, these two keen ramblers went up Ingleborough, descended into the Greta Valley and, after tea, went up Whernside and on the way home crossed Penyghent too. The walk took them 14 hours and was about 27 miles. Subsequently the thriving rambling and mountaineering clubs of the north undertook the walk and varied the actual route and reduced the time taken to complete it.

Twelve years after that first walk, members of the Yorkshire Ramblers' Club started from Gearstones above Ribblehead and completed the round in 10½ hours. By August 1926 the record time of 8 hours and 37 minutes had been recorded by the famous Pearson twins, who had started and finished at the Hill Inn, Chapel le Dale. At this time these two rugged ramblers were twelve years old! The Hill Inn became the accepted starting and finishing point for the walk, though one can quite easily start anywhere as it is a circuit. The other two favourite points are Ribblehead and Horton-in-Ribblesdale. The latter is a good place as one is quite soon on Penyghent, a rough track leading up towards it from the village. The most interesting feature at Horton is the old, bleak church which was erected about A.D. 1100 and is dedicated to Saint Oswald, King of Mercia. The fine Norman archway over the south door and the Norman font with zig-zag markings are of particular interest, though the view over crooked gable-ends to Penyghent is more remarkable. Along the lane leading up to Horton-in-Ribblesdale from Stainforth the hill—I will revert to calling it a mountain as it certainly deserves that title—is dramatic, all the more so with the shimmering grey of limestone visible half-way up the western face. It is *the* English Suilven, a peak with outstanding profile and *the* peak of the Pennines. Only three other summits come close to sharing the glory—the glory of form and not of absolute altitude—and they are neighbouring Ingleborough, Pendle Hill to the south and Shutlingsloe on the western border of the Peak District.

Walking developed into running, and each year since 1954 this event has been held in April. By 1960 the fantastic time of 2 hours 58 minutes and 45 seconds had been recorded by Frank Dawson of Salford. Walking and running are two different things; the former undertaken for enjoyment of the hills, while the latter is primarily for the pleasure of the physical hardship of running. Perhaps we walkers should hold our counsel and leave the Three Peaks runners to enjoy themselves on one Sunday in the year, but I cannot help thinking that such an organized undertaking is a mild form of desecration of the natural peace of the Craven hills. However, it is not so ludicrous as the annual Three Peaks Cyclo-Cross, which entails the covering of the Three Peaks route on, or carrying, a bicycle. The first cyclo-cross was held in 1961 and, perhaps surprisingly, the record time is longer than that held by running. Whether a cyclist will ever complete the circuit in a shorter time than the record running time seems doubtful, for it is inevitable that on the steepest and roughest ground—as up to the summit of Ingleborough and Whernside—the cyclist must shoulder his machine and so be at a definite disadvantage which cannot apparently be made up on the level and downhill sections.

Organized exhibitionism seems to be the order of the day among certain sections of the urban community, and the Three Peaks have seen, besides runners and cyclists competing against the clock, an army team driving a Land-Rover over the route in under twelve hours. Harry Watson has written that "the true fell walker must abhor this sort of activity", and with that all lovers of the countryside will agree. I see no harm in attempting to cycle over wild country or, even, to take a motor-cycle on to lonely hills. What is disgusting is the mass-invasion and the spirit of competition which organized racing against the clock and man-against-man brings to these wonderful places where Nature has held sway in beautiful harmony for so long. The runners and cyclists will disappear in time, but the fell-wanderer will remain, with time enough to enjoy these three hills, their flanks and the life upon them.

Ribblehead Viaduct

CHAPTER IX

DARK HILLS OF HEATHER

SOUTH of the Aire Gap millstone grit becomes king, predominating as the surface rock for 35 miles to the limestone plateau of the Peak District, the White Peak. On both sides of the high moorland ridge (and its many branching spurs between deep troughs) the industria of eastern Lancashire and the West Riding—cotton and woollens—press hard. Over the period from the Industrial Revolution, since coal took over from water as the major source of power, the tall-rising chimneys have belched their pollution over these Pennine hills and darkened the already-shaded heather and bilberry and the rock tors of millstone grit. More so than is often realized, the soot of eastern Lancashire has darkened these heather hills, blown by the prevailing westerly winds; a large proportion of the West Riding's smoke and soot has drifted eastwards, away from the hills and only pollutes their flanks locally (as about Halifax and Todmorden).

Only occasionally does the main Pennine ridge in this region attain shapeliness, and the outstanding hill of the district between Craven and the Peak District is, without doubt, Pendle (1,831 feet). This conspicuous and relatively isolated hill-shape lies off the main ridge, over to the west between the Rossendale Hills to the south and mid-Ribblesdale, well inside Lancashire. To those who believe that Yorkshire takes the lion's share of the central Pennines all I can say is that in this latitude Lancashire makes up with quality what it lacks in quantity, for the high, rolling moors, the deep lanes and pretty, stone-built villages about Pendle cannot be bettered anywhere. The focal point of this Lancastrian hill-region is "the grey, hooded witch" of Pendle, around it gathered

Ingleborough from Gearstones

several rewarding valleys and many unspoilt settlements—like Wycoller and Downham. This is real witch country, too. The name Pendle is synonymous with witchcraft, notably in late medieval and subsequent times. In fact, witches were numerous in this remote part of the north country until 1612, when the Lancashire witches of that period were put to trial at Lancaster. Alice Nutter and several other women of the district were found guilty of having caused the deaths of sixteen people resident in the Forest of Pendle and were put to death. After that time the evil shadows of Alice and Mother Demdike passed from the area, and Pendle became less frightening of aspect.

Today the hill, though well under 2,000 feet in height, looms large when seen from any point of the compass. For most ramblers it has a special character, an atmosphere about it reminiscent of that shadowed past, and I remember that on my first walk up to the flat top, on a dark February day, that sinister air was particularly noticeable. There is a particularly good view of Pendle from the steep lane which descends into the village of Barley. It rears as a great, brown whale-back, and the pair of steep tracks slanting steeply up to the summit accentuate the characteristic wedge shape. On a bright, spring day when I was going down into Barley, there were people on top, clearly visible through binoculars and backed by fine, white-piled wool-packs of cumulus.

It is easy to condemn Lancashire as a county ruined by industrialization, but such wholesale criticism would certainly give an inaccurate impression. There are parts of eastern Lancashire, in the Pennine country, which are real jewels. All I need say is, do not condemn this district until you have visited Barley and Downham and the Rossendale Hills. Here is a land in complete contrast to the blackened, woollen valleys on the eastern slopes in this same latitude. Take the area beyond Brierfield and Padiham, for instance; small woods and scattered, tree-girt farms predominate, with Pendle frowning beyond. Lapwings dip over the trotting lambs, and larks and meadow-pipits are often heard in active song.

Not far away is Downham, the prettiest village in Lancashire. It is well described in that notable historical work by Harrison Ainsworth called *Lancashire Witches*. At Downham one feels the same sort of overwhelming presence of Pendle which is noted at Barley, on the eastern side of the hill. Here originated the notable Barley family who had connections with equally notable Derbyshire families. Robert Barley was the first husband of Bess of Hardwick, and a Robert Barley is buried with his wife beneath incised alabaster slabs in Barlow Parish Church (died 1467). He was of the same family.

By the main street of the village is Wilkinson's Farm, formerly a Roman Catholic chapel. The original chapel building is easily recognized and now used as farm buildings. Adjoining it is the present farmhouse with its low, beamed ceilings, and it is likely that many materials used here came from the chapel. The old farmer here recalled to me the turf-cutting on Pendle, for the farmers and cottagers of Barley had—and still have—the right to take away turf from the open hillsides. The rights are set down in their deeds but few, if any, individuals bother to dig and cart the turves from the hill these days. There are allotments, too, on Pendle; not garden allotments but fields made by dividing open land where farmers have grazing rights according to ancient agreements.

Close to Barley is Whitehough. There is a farm and a Youth Hostel here, and there is now a camp school owned by the Lancashire Education Authority. For many years these camp schools have taken groups of schoolchildren from the adjoining industrial areas and introduced them to wild places, giving them a much needed breath of fresh air. My good friend Kenneth Oldham is the headmaster at Whitehough Camp School, and in his care the visiting groups get to know the thrills of camping in the hills, the wild life of the Pennines and something of the many activities which man can enjoy there; rambling, rock climbing and potholing. Kenneth Oldham was with me on Ruwenzori in central Africa, and his enthusiasm for and knowledge of wild places cannot be bettered. As a professional ciné photographer his fame has spread far and wide. Here, then, is a good use to which the Pennines can be put; as a wonderful outdoor laboratory and place for intelligent amusement.

The well-known Yorkshire writer and photographer, G. Bernard

Wood, has recently stated that "Wycoller must be saved for posterity. It is integral to the Pennine ethos." What is of particular interest there? It is, like many of the remoter places of the northern hills which are too far from urban areas to be spoilt by invasion by towny folks (who believe that they are improving a village or a single cottage by spending lavishly on it and by so doing destroy the original taste and the spirit of the place, usually simply functional and 'local' because it was conceived locally). No, Wycoller simply fell into disuse, though for 200 years (during the seventeenth and eighteenth centuries) it had been a centre of handloom weaving. The ruins of the great house, the home of the notable Cuncliffes for a long period, stand nearby and were partly restored by the Friends of Wycoller. This group of interested persons has now ceased to function, but through their hard work the attractions of the village were broadcast and partly restored. It is an easy step now from this western flank of the central Pennines to the more famous eastern flank, and the Mecca must surely be Haworth on its hill overlooking the murky Worth Valley.

Everyone knows that Haworth goes with the Brontë family, and volumes have been written about them and their Pennine associations. They are, especially the three sisters, *the* literary characters of the Pennines, and their works are largely Pennine. They ranged far and wide in their walks and drives in this hill country and used many, many situations (suitably disguised) in their works. I suppose Charlotte Brontë was the most widely travelled of the three sisters, using situations she had experienced over a considerable area of the Pennines in her stories. *Jane Eyre*, for instance, ranges far for typical settings, and Charlotte took her "Ferndean Manor" from Wycoller Hall, the great house of that Lancashire village already mentioned above and about seven miles west of Haworth. On a visit to Hathersage, where she stayed with the vicar of this lovely Peakland village, Charlotte found Moorseats Hall on the steep hill above the church and made this the home of the kindly Rivers family. It is often thought that she chose part of the house as a setting for the Rochester household, too; a house with a locked door, behind which the sinister Mrs. Rochester was kept.

Even when the Brontës came to Haworth in April 1820 there were about 1,200 handlooms still in use in the district, but there had been, and was still to come, much trouble between workers and employers as power looms were introduced to the new mills. The parsonage and the parish church are sited well up the hill, above the 750-feet contour, so subsequent development has largely taken place below the old village, with its steep, narrow street and stone buildings on various levels. The heart of Haworth has, in fact, remained and lies close to the open country which starts over the graveyard wall. The land rises up to Hill Top and beyond to the heather moors which are popularly linked with the Brontë family.

There is insufficient space here to detail all the lovely moorland features near Haworth, but two houses are outstanding, both with Brontë associations. One is the derelict farm called Top Withens about 3 miles west of Haworth. The best way is to leave the village by West Lane and go by way of the famous (though sometimes over-rated) Brontë Falls on the Sladen Beck. Beyond this little fall of water climb by derelict Virginian Farm and so to the Stanbury to Withens Lane. The lonely farm called Top Withens stands in a ruinous state overlooking the blue distances of the Worth Valley and the moors running above Oakworth to Keighley. Incidentally, the steep road up out of Keighley which leads to Oakworth reveals some good views (often hazy with industrial pollution) of the Aire Valley. Mill upon mill, Methodist church and tall terraces of gritstone houses. Climbing these Pennine-side slopes are scores of drab streets, like Oxford Street off the Oakworth-Keighley road, which conjure up images of wet Sunday afternoons. Top Withens, though, is away from all this forlorn detail of Victorian urban development and possesses a natural state of the neglected, of Man against wild and intolerant Nature. It is very likely that Emily Brontë modelled her "Wuthering Heights" on this hill farm. In 1964 the Brontë Society set a stone tablet upon the ruins in response to many inquiries stating that the farmhouse is associated with the house in Emily's well-known novel. It was her only novel, and it is claimed that it "stands out in the history of English literature because of its striking originality and timelessness". Another claim and one which is quite feasible is that Emily set nearby High Sunderland Hall in the environment of Top Withens. Yet another is that "Wuthering Heights" is really Ponden Hall, the other house quite close to Haworth which I have space here to mention.

Some believe that Ponden Hall is the model for "Thrushcross Grange" in that single and outstanding novel by Emily, but others have identified the rooms and outbuildings as being accurate for the farmhouse at "Wuthering Heights"; certainly the name bears more resemblance to Top Withens. Ponden Hall stands above an arm of Ponden Reservoir, sheltered by trees, and is right on the Pennine Way. In fact, it is one of the handful of places on this long-distance walking route which provides refreshments and even accommodation. It is a grand, low-built gritstone farm with mullioned windows and an attractive garden. Robert Heaton built the Hall in 1634, and it was partly rebuilt a century and a half ago. The Heatons were still living there in Brontë times, five bachelor brothers being friendly with the sisters from Haworth, though younger than them. Ponden Hall is worth travelling a long way to see; a typical central Pennine yeoman farmer's dwelling in a sound state of preservation.

To the south of the Haworth district are various moorlands—Heptonstall Moor, Chelburn Moor and others—dotted with interesting memorials consisting of plaques and some on a larger scale. The outstanding one is on Stoodley Pike, a mile and a half south of the Todmorden-Hebden Bridge road (A646). The tower rises to 120 feet above the crest of the escarpment and is very obvious in clear conditions from most points of the compass. It dominates the Calder Valley and was built to mark the abdication of Napoleon (1814) and the Peace of Ghent, a most imposing structure which draws the rambler onward along the main Pennine ridge, whether he is walking from the north or south. That atmospheric pollution has been serious up on the heights above the industrial valleys during the last century and a half is obvious if one tries to read the stone tablet on the northern face of the tower; the words are now very hard to make out. Of course, the full force of winter winds and rain at this altitude has assisted in the destruction of the tablet, but pollution from industry has caused the worse damage; damage also to the main structure, and to date it has had to be rebuilt twice!

To the south of Stoodley Pike lies much heather-clad millstone-grit moor, occupying the main watershed hereabouts between the North Sea and Irish Sea. Most of this constitutes relatively easy going for the serious walker, and the ridge is crossed at intervals by roads linking the woollen towns of the east with the cotton districts of the west. The Rochdale-Halifax road (A58) runs past the White House Inn, over 1,200 feet above sea-level, and nearby is Blackstone Edge Reservoir. From this escarpment crest there are distant and impressive views down to the west, to Littleborough, with Rochdale and the wide spread of industry on the Lancashire plain beyond. Away over several intervening crests the characteristic shape of Pendle Hill can be espied. A mile or so to the south of the White House Inn is the triangulation station on Blackstone Edge, and beyond that again the Oldham-Halifax road (A672) crosses Axletree Edge with White Hill to the south. Before gaining the top of Millstone Edge, 2½ miles to the south, the Rochdale-Huddersfield road (A640) comes over at Little Moss close to 1,400 feet above sea-level. The summit of Millstone Edge is particularly interesting for it possesses the Ammon Wrigley memorial, a large corner of millstone grit upon which commemorative details of this son of nearby Saddleworth are set down. When he died at the age of 85 in 1946 Ammon Wrigley had become well known as a true lover of the Pennine countryside through his verse and other writings. His name lives on at Millstone Edge. Less than a mile to the south again is the famous Standedge Cutting carrying the very busy Oldham-Huddersfield road (A62) over the ridge. It is interesting to remember when one stands by the Standedge Cutting that far below is the notorious Standedge canal tunnel (see Chapter II) and a pair of railway tunnels, several hundred feet underground at this point. The ancient trackways over these moorlands are a study in themselves, and much research has been done into their origin. The best way to find out about them is to read Dr. Arthur Raistrick's various books on the subject, for in them he tells the story of old routes over the hills.

The industrial towns on both flanks grew up largely because of the ample water supplies draining off the moors. The steep valleys provided the necessary power and, as the populations grew, they provided suitable impervious sites for storing drinking water. Today this part of the central Pennines is literally dotted with reservoirs supplying water to Lancashire and Yorkshire. Good examples are Huddersfield Corporation's reservoirs in the Wessenden valley near Marsden. A sheet of water can quite often add interest and charm otherwise lacking to moorland country where outstanding hill-shapes are missing, and here drifts of rhododendrons have been planted. These certainly add great attraction, especially in May and June when masses of blooms add unexpected colour to the valley. There is usually an outcry when a new reservoir is proposed, and too much water would surely take away too much attractive walking country and the natural habitats for the native flora and fauna, but, quite often, a bend in a clough-path or a rise in a moorland plateau can reveal the sudden change to water and the various secondary attractions that that can bring—water plants and water birds and man's own plantings of trees and flowering shrubs.

A tradition grew up long ago for most woollen mills of the West Riding to have their own brass bands and these are synonymous with the central Pennine valleys. Take, for instance, the mills of Messrs. Foster at Queenbury, near Halifax. These are called the Black Dyke Mills, and there has been a thriving brass band associated with these mills since 1816. Even the music stands which are used are one hundred years old. This tradition lives on, if not quite so vigorously as twenty years ago, and Lancashire has similar brass bands, the main aim of which seems to be competition one band with another for perfection of playing in much the same way as singing and verse at eisteddfodau in Wales.

The lie of the land has prevented many of the West Riding towns from being dull in a way so common in the Midlands. Steep streets and jostling buildings in native stone are often attractive and always fascinating. Quite close to the very centres of industrial towns one can come upon pockets of relatively unspoilt country with ancient farmhouses and cottages. Barkisland is such a place, on a steep hillside between Elland and Ripponden. The old cottages are blackened gritstone with remarkably pale pointing between. The pavement of worn flagstones is typically West Riding, and beside the former police station are the stocks, a relic of former days and cruder justice. The Griffin Inn, half-way up the main street, dates from 1642, and some way below it are the most important—and impressive—buildings of the village. One is Knowlson House, a Tudor farmhouse in the typical West Riding architecture of the period; below it is the well-cared-for Lower Hall, and next is the gateway to Barkisland Hall. This is one of the finest small mansions of the Pennines and stands at the upper end of a short drive overhung by large deciduous trees. The imposing circular window on the front of the hall is the feature which immediately strikes the observer, but the whole building is finely proportioned and was obviously the pride of land and mill-owners of the past.

Another interesting building of this region is Ashday Hall, Southowram, near Halifax. It dates from a later period (built between 1713 and 1738) than Barkisland Hall and can be compared with the latter to show the evolution of West Riding mansions. Ashday Hall is secluded, and in its lovely gardens are many rare plants.

Before the main Pennine ridge slides southwards into the broader expanse of the Peak District proper it rises to Black Hill (1,908 feet), a mile and a half west of the television transmitting station and mast on Holme Moss. The well-known guide-book writer, A. Wainwright, has recently described Black Hill—the highest point in Cheshire, incidentally—as being "well named". He accurately states that "it is not the only fell with a summit of peat, but no other shows such a desolate and hopeless quagmire to the sky". When that same sky is obscured by low clouds Black Hill becomes really depressing, and the word "hopeless" is then very fitting. Come the spring, though, and open skies and bird song brightens the outlook. Curlews and dunlins call across this desert of peat, and occasionally one can find their nesting sites. I recall finding a lonely dunlin's nest with three eggs on nearby Upper Dead Edge one May day and being subjected to constant attack from the parents until I had left their territory.

The land hereabouts slips gently towards the south from Black Hill by way of several cloughs, the most important being Crowden Great Brook, to the trench of Longdendale. But we are now virtually in the Peak District, that part we shall call the Black Peak. All-in-all, the dark hills of heather between Craven and Peakland are full of interest for the discerning traveller on foot. To savour their charm to the full, good weather and long legs are an advantage.

CHAPTER X

MARSDEN TO EDALE

THE first one-inch tourist map of the Peak District was published by the Ordnance Survey in 1957 but did not include the far north of the National Park for practical reasons. The new edition, published in 1963, was rearranged to include the entire area of the park—from Herdman's Close Farm, near Ashbourne, in the extreme south to Deer Hill, near Marsden, in the extreme north.

Marsden lies below the little valley of Wessenden, drained by the Shiny Brook. The Pennine Alternative (a route for bad conditions which avoids the undefined wastes of White Moss) comes this way and then winds up to Standedge on the main watershed. One of the finest classic Pennine walks of all is the high-level route from Marsden to Edale, a distance of about twenty-five miles over Wessenden Moor, Black Hill, Bleaklow and Kinder Scout. It is a lovely route in good weather and a stiff exercise in bad conditions. It is to Fred Heardman of Edale that we owe the 'Double Marsden-Edale', a route of between forty-five and fifty miles and covering these high plateaux twice. This indefatigable rambler first invented and accomplished this 'double' route in the early twenties, and very few others attempted it until the fifties. It is still only completed infrequently by the hardiest of enthusiastic 'bogtrotters'. In September 1953 V. J. Desmond and E. Courtenay completed this 'double' walk in the quick time of 12 hours 55 minutes, 6 hours being taken each way, and the remaining 55 minutes being taken in rest and refreshments at Marsden.

On a fine, summer day the 'single' route from Marsden to Edale is well worth doing by any strong rambler. The first section lies, as already stated, up the clough of the Shiny Brook which dissects Wessenden Moor. The rhododendrons cluster the clough-sides in the vicinity of the celebrated waterfall, and Wessenden Lodge supplies refreshments to the picnickers who come at the week-end. Four reservoirs partially fill the bottom of the clough, but, I think, do not detract from the scenic appeal. Maybe they enhance it. The path winds up the eastern side of the waters for three miles before gaining the A635—the Barnsley-Huddersfield road—at the site of the once-famous Isle of Skye Inn, demolished on account of fears of pollution of drinking water. We are at almost 1,500 feet above sea-level now, and to the south the great, dark mass of Black Hill (1,908 feet) is guarded by the nearer sweep of Wessenden Head Moor.

To follow the line of the Pennine Way alternative route, which keeps off the highest land hereabouts and is specifically designed for use in bad conditions when visibility is poor, entails the descent into and ascent out of three eastward-facing cloughs, and, if possible, it is much better to strike to the south-west from the site of the Isle of Skye Inn and gain the gentle top of Dean Head Hill, then turn for a mile and a half south-eastwards over cloudberry expanses to the peat wastes of Black Hill. It could not be better named, especially when low cloud threatens rain, and visibility is reduced to mediocre. Here are the county boundary crosses, and the two counties involved may be a surprise to those unfamiliar with the area. To the north lies the West Riding of Yorkshire, and to the south is Cheshire. Actually this summit is the highest point in the latter county (1,908 feet) and also its northernmost point—surprisingly far north, for it is at the same latitude as Oldham and Barnsley. The television transmission mast upon Holme Moss lies over a mile to the south-east, and it is worth recalling here that J. Harvey, an outstanding Pennine walker who was one of a team of three which completed the 'Double Marsden-Edale' in December 1950 in 19 hours and in very poor weather conditions, made a secret but successful climb up the newly-erected mast. This event was later reported in the national Press and caused a severe rebuke from the British Broadcasting Corporation.

Not far from the thin vertical line of the mast is the summit of the road which crosses from Woodhead to Holmfrith, and long ago there stood an inn called 'Bill o' Jacks' where a brutal double murder was committed in 1832. Today the site is overgrown, and the lonely road swings its way down into the West Riding from Cheshire, from the 1,718-foot watershed. The usual way towards Edale is to continue southwards on the line of Tooleyshaw Moss and Westend Moss (1,729 feet) then down the narrowing shoulder, which becomes in turn Hey Moss and Hey Edge. Below on the left is the uppermost of the string of reservoirs owned by Manchester Corporation. It is called Woodhead Reservoir, filling the upper reaches of Longdendale in the district where farms, cottages and railwaymen's houses come under the general term of Woodhead. Where the Pennine Way comes down to the main road is Crowden, with its new Youth Hostel and enticing glimpses in clear weather up the clough drained by Crowden Great Brook to that most notable of all Cheshire gritstone out-crops called Laddow Rocks.

For the Marsden to Edale walker the next stage of the journey usually assumes the least-attractive countenance. Bleaklow itself is a wonderful place and with endless fascination, but when one is engaged on a high-level cross-country walk the attaining of the goal is of paramount importance, and each upland mass is a hurdle to be overcome. One is still fresh when crossing Wessenden Moor, and from Black Hill there is a general downhill trend. But then the steep, northern side of Bleaklow has to be ascended and the peat plateau crossed to the top of the Snake Pass. In low cloud a com-pass is essential, as on Black Hill. Beyond the Snake Pass there is the level of Featherbed Moss (1,785 feet) and, if one takes the direct route towards Edale and away from the Pennine Way, the drop into Ashop Clough. Now the steeper climb of Black Ashop Moor brings one on to the dark crest of The Edge, Kinder Scout's prominent northern gritstone scarp. This fine plateau is guarded on all flanks by steep gritstone 'edges', most vertical but readily by-passed by way of the bilberry and heather slopes bordering either end of each such crag. The best known are this northern Edge, Fairbrook Naze to the east, Seal Edge still further beyond and the western scarps, where the Kinder River drops to form the famous Kinder Downfall. All in all this plateau is the best known of Peakland heights and one of the principal summit regions of the Pennines; it is a sort of southern 'great top'—the last high upland of the ridge before the lesser tops lead Pennine-land down into Midland green and wooded slopes.

We have left the route of the Pennine Way, remember; and now it is a matter of traversing straight to the south by the slight ridge marked by Crowden Head (2,070 feet) and so to the head of Grinds Brook, where the Pennine Way comes in from the north-west—undefined here—and so down the steep defile of Grinds Brook Clough to the terminal fields and the log bridge above Edale. Up there, less than a mile to the south-west of Crowden Tower, is the highest point of Peakland; this insignificant rise of the heather-and-peat moor to 2,088 feet above sea-level marks more than just the highest land of the district, for it is the highest top of the Pennines south of Fountains Fell (2,191 feet), Great Whernside (2,310 feet), Penyghent (2,273 feet) and Ingleborough (2,373 feet), which lie athwart the main axis of the ridge in the Craven district. In fact, Kinder Scout is almost the highest top in England south of Craven—which is quite a distinction, consider-ing the area involved.

The 'double' Marsden-Edale walker must now turn around and face the ascent of Grinds Brook Clough, up through the trees with the perfect spire of gritstone called Ringing Roger peering through, high up on the right. The walk up the well-known track of the clough seems to take a lot longer when one is setting forth at the beginning of a day's ramble than when one has been going hard for several hours. One's pace is different then, one is 'warmed-up' for the task, and, instead of about one hour from Edale to the plateau-top, it is nearer three-quarters of an hour now. Then on across the undulations and hare-dotted, grouse-cackling moor at the 2,000-foot level. At the northern side of the plateau the first dim view of Bleaklow's main ridge is a bit demoralizing, seemingly a score of miles away and unattainable.

When one has descended again into Ashop Clough, though, and on up over Featherbed Moss, the crossing of the Snake Road brings you nearer to that ridge, and, after the rough crossing by

Devil's Dike, the Wain Stones come into sight, and soon the 2,060-foot level at Bleaklow Head is under one's feet. There before your eyes rears another distant horizon which has, of course, to be crossed. It is that dark upland culminating in Black Hill. But the descent into Longdendale is soon completed, and we cross the electrified railway line between Sheffield and Manchester, over the top of the impounding wall of Torside Reservoir and up the main road before taking to the rough ground which leads up Crowden Great Brook to that black and virtually vegetationless top of Black Hill and Wessenden Head Moor. This section of the return walk is undoubtedly the worst part, and heart is somewhat lost as altitude is gained. Only after crossing the A635 road near the Isle of Skye Inn is the end of the 'double' walk in sight, with the three-mile drop down the Wessenden Valley.

So ends a remarkable gritstone walk which has many rewards. One of the problems for the rambler is arranging transport, whether he is planning the 'single' or 'double' walk. With curtailed train services it often requires a combination of car, bus and train if one has to travel any distance to Marsden or Edale.

CHAPTER XI

THE BLACK PEAK

MOST of the breeds of Pennine sheep were—or still are—found upon the dark brown, green and yellow heights of the northern Peak District, where millstone grit is the predominant surface rock. Throughout the centuries the escarpments and the plateaux of this wonderful district have supported great flocks. Many were originally owned by monastic foundations but later passed to individuals, and today we see these flockmasters wandering the heights with their dogs.

There are no finer profiles or threatening skies in the whole of the Pennine region than those to be found here in the gritstone region near the southern terminal of the ridge. Take the northward view from Back Tor, one of the highest points (1,765 feet) of the great escarpment forming Derwent Edge overlooking the upper Derwent Valley on its eastern side. Away to the north the great hollow of the Abbey Brook acts as a foreground for the heights, sweeping lonely and graceful towards the ever-present clouds on the last horizon—heights with lovely names which could only be Pennine; Featherbed Moss, Margery Hill and Outer Edge. Across these northern heights the ancient trackway crossing from Penistone into Derwent Dale is invisible; it is the famous Cut Gate used by farmers and drovers over many centuries.

Down there the Abbey Brook winds steeply westwards into Derwent Dale, a deeply incised stream with a significant name. Though the name Derwent did not appear in any of the records connected with the Domesday Survey, land was acquired by the Canons of Welbeck Abbey during the twelfth century, and an abbey grange was founded near the mouth of the Abbey Clough;

Gordale Scar

this survives even to this present time as Abbey Farm. The monks of the abbey grange built, among other things, four wayside chapels in this area, but none remain. The same fate befell the two bridges they erected over the River Derwent; the one upstream from the village of Derwent was replaced by Ouzleden Bridge, which was subsequently submerged when the Derwent Reservoir was built in 1916. The second bridge was for packhorses and crossed the river in the valley; by the latter half of the seventeenth century the bridge was in a very dilapidated condition and was rebuilt by one Henry Balguy, whose family originated in the Hope Valley. He it was who built the beautiful Derwent Hall in 1672. The Newdigates sold the Hall to the Duke of Norfolk, and in this way a great area of the hills above Derwent Dale came into the possession of that family. In 1932 the Hall became a Youth Hostel and finally disappeared for ever beneath the waters of the Ladybower Reservoir, opened in September 1945. The third reservoir filling the floor of Derwent Dale is the uppermost, called Howden, which was the first to be completed by the Derwent Valley Water Board (in 1912) to supply the towns of Derby, Nottingham and Leicester. Much has been written of the flooding of this wild dale, and Dr. Mary Andrews's poignant description in *Long Ago in Peakland* of a visit to forsaken Derwent Hall on a summer evening in 1938 is especially memorable.

Derwent Dale nowadays normally refers to the upper valley drained by Derbyshire's largest river, the steep-sided dale above its confluence with the River Ashop at the centre of the present Ladybower Reservoir. Formerly, however, the name was used to describe a greater portion of the valley-system. The earliest known reference to Derwent Dale as such is in John of Gaunt's Register (1379–83), and subsequently the Woolley Charters of 1473. Above these upper reaches are numerous romantically sited farms with long and fascinating histories. Take Lockerbrook Farm on the long, south-pointing ridge which separates the lower Woodlands and Derwent Dales; a place known in the thirteenth century as Lokebroc and later to become Locbroc and Lochbrock. William Senior referred to the place in 1627 by its modern name, a name quite probably meaning 'a brook by an enclosure'. Take, also,

7

Pennine farmer at Barley, Lancashire

finely-placed and proportioned Rowlee Farm above the Wood-lands Valley and long-submerged Ronksley Farm and derelict Abbey Farm. Hereabouts are numerous other farmsteads, stand-ing lonely on their hillsides, never upon the crests of these high and unproductive heights. There are Two Thorn Fields, Gillethey, Hayridge, Upper Ashop and Hagg Farms; the latter standing typically where instability of the surface shales has caused much crumbling and looking southwards to the bold brow of Crookstone Knoll, which forms the easternmost crest of the Kinder Scout massif across the Woodlands Valley. High above the farm are remnants of the oak-woods which once covered a great part of this high valley and gave it the name by which it has been known since at least as early as 1577, when C. Saxton produced his first map of Derbyshire.

On a warm and bright Saturday in late March I followed one of my favourite routes in the Black Peak—from the road-head at Ronksley up the highest reaches of Derwent Dale to the very source of the river above Swains Greave, at 1,900 feet above sea-level. The previous few days had been gloriously warm—unsea-sonably so—and we took our time as we followed the left bank of the rapidly lessening river in its torrent stage. Ahead of us a long, dark object appeared, disappeared and re-appeared among the heather and rushes; my friend's unlikely rambling companion was a four-year-old dachshund bitch which, despite her apparent physical disadvantages was a good goer in rough country and always completed the day in front of the party.

There were a few lambs about on the slopes above us, and their calls, so evocative of the hills of spring, mingled with those of the first curlews, which had already flown up from their estuarine mud-flats where they had over-wintered and were now seeking suitable nesting sites.

One of the pleasures of Pennine rambling is the surprise encounters with others of like mind. On this particular day Melvin and I lunched with a man from Surrey who was breaking his business trip to the north for a day or two on the heights. We ate above the narrow gorge where the infant Derwent cuts down steeply from a nick-point after draining the relatively level area of Swains Greave. As we ate, I recalled a torrid summer afternoon long ago, when Stewart, David and I had paddled here in the gorge, when the rocks radiated the terrific heat and finally drove us on to Swains Greave.

The most important Derbyshire and Peak District river is the Derwent. In this lonely, north-facing hollow one is shut off from the world, a sort of desert basin with only the short slopes of heather and grasses and the sky for company. Now and again the mountain hares, conspicuous in spring and early autumn with their white coats, move across these slopes; the red grouse come gliding into view off the plateau-top and call loudly as they go. But even three centuries ago Swains Greave was a very different sort of place, as the name suggests. The place was 'Swaines graue head' in 1627, and this suggests 'a copse'—a copse or woodland grove in this inhospitable place? Look in the exposed layers of peat and underlying soil where the river has cut deeply at Swains Greave. Here are well preserved birch branches, the bark often intact. Peat has built up, soil conditions have become acid, and the trees have slowly died, much in the same way as the trees of Hoo Moor above the Goyt Valley are dying today. Now there are no trees overshadowing the uppermost reaches of the Derwent.

From the 1,900-foot levels above the Barrow Stones and the Grinah Stones one looks south and west over the only desert in our islands; a cold, tundra-like desert dissected with those fine and deep troughs of the Westend, Alport and Ashop Valleys. Beyond lies the rectangular blue form of Kinder Scout (2,088 feet), the highest point of Peakland and the southern Pennines—classical example of a plateau, a far more popular area than the heights of Bleaklow where we now stand.

Whereas most of Kinder Scout above the 2,000-feet contour exhibits eroded common cotton-grass (*Eriophorum angustifolium*), vegetation cover with bilberry surrounding it at a lower level above about 1,500 feet, the predominant plants on Bleaklow are species of ling above 2,000 feet, and only on the north-facing slopes above 1,750 feet is eroded *Eriophorum* dominant—this time not common cotton-grass but the more tussocky harestail (*Eriop-horum vaginatum*). Here may be a good place to discuss the natural vegetation cover of the Pennine region as a whole.

Of the common native tree species of these heights the ash occurs mainly in connection with the Carboniferous limestone. In some districts these ashwoods are definitely natural and are best seen in parts of the 'White' Peak District, where limestone outcrops on the surface. The Pennine oak-woods occur on hillsides formed from non-calcareous rocks of the Carboniferous series, rocks exemplified by the Yoredale shales, millstone grit and coal measures. These woods attain about 900 feet above sea-level and are dominated by the Durmast or Sessile oak (*Quercus sessili-flora*); the canopy formed by the upper branches is not normally closed (or forming a complete, tree-top cover). The shrub layer of other, smaller plants is not normally very luxuriant, and where the woods are at quite a high altitude the dominant plants upon the ground are creeping soft-grass and bracken.

So much for the woods, which, of course, do not form very extensive features of these hills. According to Sir A. G. Tansley, one of the foremost botanists in the world, the word 'moss' is the commonest place name of the Pennines, and the cotton-grass bogs —or mosses as they are always known—are typical of all the region. These mosses occupy level areas of poor drainage between 1,000 feet and 2,200 feet above sea-level. The common cotton-grass (*Eriophorum angustifolium*) or the harestail (*Eriophorum vaginatum*) is often the only important plant growing in wide areas where peat-beds are found, beds which may reach thirty feet in depth. The latter species is usually found in drier peat, especially in the southern Pennines. Large areas of the northern Pennines consist of mixed communities of cotton-grass and ling, and above the 2,000-feet contour the communities contain bil-berry too. Ling will tolerate a wide variation in the water content of the soil, and research has shown that the purer the peat the more water ling can tolerate.

Besides these cotton-grass bogs, the higher, uncultivated land supports two other types of plant community—bilberry moor and

heather moor. In the northern Pennines ling tends to disappear
above 2,000 feet, and the vegetation is dominated by bilberry
(*Vaccinium myrtillus*), cowberry, (*Vaccinium vitis-idaea*), heath rush
(*Juncus squarrosus*) and mat-grass (*Nardus stricta*). This pattern is also
to be seen at the higher levels of the southern Pennines in West
Yorkshire, bilberry occupying the highest tops of the lower hills
with an altitude of between 1,400 and 1,700 feet. The dominance
of bilberry seems to be determined by greater exposure and better
drainage compared with the heather moors occupying the slopes
below. On the steeper, rocky slopes below many of the cotton-
grass mosses of plateaux like Bleaklow colonies of bilberry are
found, and the flora is often quite rich because of the greater
shelter. Even individual birch trees and bracken are found.

The heather moors of the Pennines are among the very best in
England and reach as low as 750 feet in the south, though normally they occupy an altitude band between 1,000 and 1,500 feet
above sea-level. In the northern Pennines this upper limit extends
sometimes to 2,000 feet, but at higher altitudes the species loses its
dominance in favour of 'blanket bog' or 'moss'.

A word here about an interesting feature; the boundary
between heather and grassland. Adamson showed in 1918 that the
upper limit of natural grassland coincides with the lower limit of
heather, that there is a reasonably sudden break between the two
floral types. He also showed that if grazing was concentrated the
grass invaded the heather, and if grazing stopped the heather
invaded the grassland.

The Black Peak extends in an arc around the limestone, and surprisingly large areas of Cheshire and Staffordshire are within this
region. Some of these western heights are conspicuous and beautiful in form—take, for instance, that most lovely of Peakland hills
called Shutlingsloe (1,659 feet), overlooking the deep cleft of
Wildboarclough five miles south-east of Macclesfield; then there
is the witch-like grotesqueness of the Roaches across the border in
Staffordshire, a bold gritstone escarpment which is popular as a
climbing ground and has many difficult routes. Shining Tor
(1,834 feet) overlooks the A537 above the Cat and Fiddle Inn, and

away to the north are the really wild moorlands above Longdendale, most of the tops being shared by Yorkshire's West Riding
and Cheshire as far as Holme Moss and Upper Dead Edge. Here,
upon this lonely boundary or frontier between a county normally
thought of as lush and lowland and a county associated with our
Pennines, there are many romantic names which could only be
found in this enchanting hill-country—Windgate Edge, Blind-
stones, Black Chew Head and Black Hill (at 1,908 feet the highest
point in Cheshire).

All the lovely Black Peak of gritstone escarpments and peaty
groughs, well-watered cloughs and sudden plateau-edge views
over distant, smoky lowlands east and west is the realm of the true
rambler. The faint-heart and artificial town-dweller, who has
never wished to wander upon these hills so relatively close at
hand, is to be pitied. He who does not know the sting of Pennine
hail upon the cheek or the swirl of damp cloud which sticks to the
clothing or the fierce rays of a June sun on high in these high
places has missed a large slice of real life, and what on this earth
has he to look back on with a burning and longing and smiling
heart? What can carry him through the lonely and saddest hours
if remembrances of Featherbed Top or Alport Dale are not his
share?

Mention of Alport Dale reminds me that at the time of writing
there are suggestions afoot that a new reservoir to be built somewhere in Peakland may be planned to fill this loveliest of all
remote cloughs of the southern Pennines; here or in Ashop
Clough which contains the infant River Ashop. That such suggestions for an established National Park must be taken seriously
is a shocking reflection on 'the powers', the 'Philistines' who for
sheer 'economic' or 'amenity' reasons are willing to ruin for all
time this wonderful territory. Look at the transgressions in the
Snowdonia National Park in connection with the Trawsfynydd
nuclear power station of the Central Electricity Generating
Board—if it can happen at the wild heart of that National Park it
can happen in Alport Dale or in Ashop Clough. It must not happen, and all sensible, sensitive countrygoers and country lovers
must make it their business to prevent such an outrage. There are

numerous less-wild valleys in Peakland which could be utilized, but there are few really wild valleys left, few lonely troughs where one can walk in almost silent conditions and see virtually no evidence of man's constructive or destructive works. Alport Dale possesses the relics of an isolated agricultural settlement, three of Peakland's finest waterfalls (features rare in this district) and Britain's biggest landslip. From the northern ramparts of Kinder Scout one looks down into the wide trough of Ashop Clough, where the water runs down from Ashop Head and Mill Hill towards the Woodlands Valley and Derwent Dale. The Council for the Preservation of Rural England will, I know, take up the fight to defend these unspoilt depressions if the suggestions become firm plans.

It was to the gritstone edges of Peakland that the first rock climbers came, braving the fury of jealous landowners and their enthusiastic gamekeepers. In 1891 J. W. Puttrell and W. J. Watson climbed the Primitive Route on Nether Tor on Kinder Scout. On the adjoining crag of Upper Tor they did the easier 30-foot ascent of Promontory Groove. A year earlier Puttrell had examined the long, west-facing scarp slope of Stanage Edge, one of the modern meccas of climbing on gritstone. Other crags explored early in this century included Laddow Rocks above Longdendale in north-east Cheshire; the Black Rocks, above Cromford; and Wharncliffe Crags, above the industry of Deepcar and Stocksbridge north of Sheffield, where the climber is ensured of becoming caked in grime from the rocks.

The rambling movement, which became so popular between the wars, was centred upon Manchester and Sheffield. A large number of enthusiastic ramblers have long been found in the industrial centres bordering the Black Peak, and details of some of the fascinating routes covered by these personalities are too numerous to describe here—routes like the Colne to Rowsley and Marsden to Edale Double. The name that comes immediately to mind is Fred Heardman of Edale, who invented so many of the great routes over the expansive heights of gritstone Peakland and beyond.

Since World War II the great rise in rock-climbing standards can be attributed directly to the techniques required to climb successfully on millstone grit—the rounded holds, the holdless cracks and the tiny ledges. The great pioneers of modern rock-climbing in this country—Joe Brown, Don Whillans, Peter Crew and the rest of a notable group—were born close to the Peak District, and here they developed their technique upon rock which was uncompromising and always steep. Because of this early experience the great gritstone cragsmen have always found climbing on greater faces in Snowdonia, the Lake District, Scotland and overseas easier; they have thereby raised their climbing standards. It is interesting to conjecture how high rock-climbing standards in other parts of Britain would be had these men never had the opportunity to explore the edges and tors of the Black Peak.

This part of the Pennines is unlike any other—it is not to be confused with the greater heights of Cross Fell, nor with the shapely giants of Craven, nor with the high fells above the Yorkshire Dales. It is a wilderness of solitude unlike any other, and we must hope that it will never be changed by the thoughtless efforts of mere man.

CHAPTER XII

THE WHITE PEAK

THE island of Carboniferous limestone which is virtually surrounded by millstone grit in the southern Pennines and forms the
white plateau-and-dale country of Peakland is not so extensive as
the similar area of countryside making up the Craven district of
the central Pennines. Dry valleys, crags and pot-holes, caves and
an abundant flora; high, level areas of predominantly limestone
crossed by ragged white dry-stone walls; copses and small, often
picturesque, villages—these are some of the features shared by
Craven and the White Peak.

South of Rushup Edge, that shaley height between Castleton
and Chapel en le Frith, the limestone slides into sudden view out
of the Black Peak. The great white scar upon Eldon Hill is plainly
seen from Rushup Edge, an unsightly limestone quarry so typical
of many in the area to the south. And within a couple of square
miles the countryside asserts itself as truly limestone; there is
immediately south of Rushup Edge the impressive Giant's Hole, a
cave system with a length of over $2\frac{1}{4}$ miles and classed as "super
severe" in standard of difficulty. A glance at the 1-inch Ordnance
Survey map shows the presence of many old mines in this region,
and most of these were constructed for the extraction of various
mineral ores. Lead has been mined in the Pennines from Roman
times, and production reached its peak between 1750 and 1800.
The most important lead ore is galena (lead sulphide), which is
found in 'rakes', or vertical veins; 'pipes,' or elongated ore masses;
in 'flats', occurring as deposits along beds of limestone; and in
'random bodies'. Fluorspar and barytes are other products of the
lead-zinc deposits in the region and are nowadays worked from

old heaps and from a few re-opened mines. One variety of fluorspar is the renowned 'Blue John', which occurs in small quantities throughout the district but in greater quantity at Treak Cliff above Castleton. The quantity of this exotic spar is very limited, and objects made from it in former times are very valuable. Quite recently I saw a pair of Adam Vase candlesticks, with ormolu sconces and stands measuring 9 inches high, sold at an auction for the world record price of £1,100.

Here and there the limestone is very weak and allowed igneous material to reach the surface, cool and solidify. These igneous rocks are known locally as 'toadstones' and are found in depressions because they weather quite rapidly. At Grange Mill, south of Winster, is an important volcanic neck of 'toadstone', and there are well-known volcanic tuffs in the valley of the River Amber at Ashover.

The limestone country extends southwards into south Derbyshire, to be overlain again by millstone grit and, in the extreme south, by the recent Keuper and Bunter sandstones of the north Midlands in the Trent Valley.

It is sad to record that for me, and others well known to me, this white land is somewhat forlorn and melancholy. The white walls extend over the green pastures to isolated copses and hidden cliffs and bleakly-sited villages. The great charm is off the plateau areas and in the hidden dales when the summer sun is shining. Dovedale, the Manifold Valley and Lathkill Dale are the best-known and more beautiful than any counterparts in the Craven limestone district.

Walk down the valley of the River Dove in late spring or early summer from Hartington, and one will never be disappointed. The valley closes in at that section called Wolfscote Dale, and here there is much bare rock and short grass ranging up the steep slopes from the clear-running stream, one of the finest trout streams in the country, where Charles Cotton and Isaac Walton sported three centuries ago and the atmosphere of which river Cotton captured so well in verse. His spirit still lives on and

My river still through the same channel glides,
Clear from the tumult, salt and dirt of tides . . . .

Downstream the dale becomes thickly wooded, and Milldale becomes Dovedale proper south of the impressive Dove Holes, water-worn hollows of considerable size above the left bank of the river. Dovedale should be visited on a quiet day in early summer, preferably not on a Saturday afternoon or Sunday. The place is a gorge beset with all the fairy charm of trees hiding corners and turrets of white limestone, pinnacles and minarets pierce the secret bowers of yew and ash and beech. The river runs dark and cool, and voles, trout and moorhens appear and disappear between mossy rocks or islands. Violets and bluebells gather in ranks up these wooded steeps, after the celandines and wood sorrel have faded. The arum lily beckons from the wild garlick beds, and butterbur spreads its immense leaves over the water's edge; meadowsweet later flowers in creamy umbels, and its heady aroma scents the dale and seems to reach to the tree-tops and the sky.

On a hot day the limestone valleys can become oppressive and drive me up on to the plateau, where the orchids flower in many damp places—common spotted orchid, bee orchid, lady orchid and others. In a damp hollow above Dovedale I know, too, of a colony of that rare musk called blood-drop emlets (*Mimulus luteus*), the yellow two-lipped flowers splashed with brilliant spots of red. The wild plant life is one of the most fascinating features of this area of the Peak District.

Another feature, as in other limestone districts, is the phenomena of disappearing water courses. The example *par excellence* hereabouts is the River Manifold, which rises close to the source of the River Dove upon the eastern slopes of Axe Edge and enters its limestone valley, soon to discard its stony river-bed to sink underground in all but very wet seasons. The river re-emerges at Ilam some miles down-stream, at a point beneath Ilam Hall (now a Youth Hostel) and within a mile of its confluence with the Dove.

Early man found life on the limestone plateaux more amenable than that in the forested valleys and wild millstone grit hills around. The ground was relatively level and suitable, with little effort, for grazing and cultivation; he kept out of the wooded hollows to a great extent. Today the White Peak still reveals its ancient past and pre-historic remains abound. Tumuli or burial mounds and chambered cairns—as at Minning Low near Taddington—and stone circles are to be found throughout the area. Arbor Low is as impressive an enigmatic stone circle as Stonehenge, though in a different way; low limestone blocks, seeming to grow out of the green sward and crouching low against an ever-living sky; a wide skyscape stretching horizonwards to the dales of the Dove and the Manifold one way and towards the gritstone uplands in every other direction. Many visitors to this historic site fail to see or feel the impact of the place, largely because they do not walk to the south-west and investigate the burial chamber called Gib Hill. From this place look back and see it in relation to the circle, walk back towards Arbor Low and try to appreciate the geometrical relationship of these tumuli complexes and their simple form as a single unit devised by clever men of a past age, who worshipped upon a plateau basically unaltered through the passage of the centuries.

Upon Beeston Tor, overlooking the left bank of the River Manifold, close to the place where the River Hamps joins it, there are a number of interesting cave entrances. One is the entrance to Saint Bertram's Cave and it extends for 600 feet. The entrance once had a door, and by several muddy scrambles one can finally squeeze out of a 'window' high up on the Tor and look down into the light of the valley. Whether Saint Bertram ever lived here is not known, though the place has obviously been a place of safety long ago, as is shown by the several archaeological remains found in the cave, among them a collection of Saxon coins.

Later came the monasteries, to set up useful farm units upon this good land. If we take a look at an Ordnance Survey map of the region, it is not long before we have made a list of 'granges'— Mouldridge Grange, Benty Grange, Roystone Grange and so on —the farms owned and managed by medieval monastic foundations in areas distant from the mother abbey or monastery.

To one, Ash Grange above Lathkill Dale, came the monks of Roche Abbey in Yorkshire. The chapel where the lay brothers worshipped before and after their day's work on the land has disappeared, but at nearby Meadow Place Grange the chapel remained as a farm building well into the nineteenth century. Between the twelfth and sixteenth centuries the system of granges was the cornerstone of the thriving woollen industry. J. W. Allen has pointed out that the name 'grange' originally described an area of land and not a building; it was outlying land given to a monastery and too far from it for the lay brothers to travel daily, so that farmhouses and outbuildings were established. The point of importance to notice is that the grange system was free from the inevitable restrictions of the serf labour and the three-field system associated with medieval village life. The granges were almost ranches, where the sheep were managed extensively, not confined.

Many of the granges have disappeared, but occasionally we find their remains, as in Monk Dale, where the foundations of a grange chapel can be located beneath undergrowth, all that is left of a grange of Lenton Abbey. Most of the granges on this limestone plateau had their own pond or mere. The one behind Mouldridge Grange is in a particularly sound state, and one can wonder at the ingenuity of the monks, for few of these meres were fed by surface drainage, though some undoubtedly had a good spring nearby. It is probable that the site of the grange was to some extent governed by the availability of water. A pond was constructed which would be kept filled by a combination of a spring supply and the 'dew pond' principle—the condensation of water on a small, circular, concrete-lined basin frequently seen nowadays on the dry, limestone plateau of this district.

Not all the granges were located upon this relatively bare upland. Some religious houses had their outlying farm estate in the gritstone area of Peakland; Welbeck Abbey, for instance, had a grange in the deep confines of Derwent Dale, referred to in the previous chapter.

More recently the limestone district of the Peak District has had a number of unlikely associations. Take, for example, the little house called Mountain Cottage, above Middleton-by-Wirksworth, where D. H. Lawrence and his wife, Frieda, came in 1918 to live for a year. This place, high up on the plateau and looking into the wooded gorge beneath, was virtually "the last domestic fortress that the Lawrences' were to hold in England". His favourite walk down the fields to Cromford by the River Derwent has barely altered in the intervening half-century, and it is with a spirit of melancholy that we follow in his footsteps over the forlorn limestone land and recall this period of unhappiness and illness and occasional relief in contentment. The atmosphere typifies the whole of this bleached and porous plateau-land.

CHAPTER XIII

THE PENNINES' END

In a general way the southern Pennines slide down and out into central Derbyshire and have their ending relatively insignificantly in southern Peakland. Carboniferous limestone takes over from millstone grit and is overlain by the young sediments associated with the Midland Plain. In the very south-western corner of the Peak District the conspicuous ridge running from north-west to south-east and known as the Weaver Hills—well inside Staffordshire—can be thought of as the south-western terminal of the Backbone of England. A better finishing post, a more outstanding ending to all that country through which we have, of necessity, travelled only scantily in this book, is the long tongue of high, gritstone country which separates the Derbyshire Derwent Valley from the coal-measure country to the east. It is known collectively as Eastmoor and extends for forty or so miles from the Penistone moors to Crich Hill in central Derbyshire. Throughout its entire length a steep, or scarp, slope is presented to the west overlooking the Derwent Valley and a relatively easy dip slope to the east, cut into by a number of streams and lying today as beautiful east-west valleys, drained by such waters as the Ewden Beck, the River Loxley, River Rivelin and River Sheaf, the Barlow Brook and Linacre Brook and the River Hipper and the Amber. Much of this territory is high heather moor or cotton-grass moss, notably southwards as far as Beeley Moor above the parklands of Chatsworth. To the south the country is largely cultivated farmland right over the crest of the escarpment, over 1,000 feet above sea-level.

If Eastmoor is one of the gems of Pennine-country (and I

believe it is), then the gems of Eastmoor are the lonely heights of the northern crest and the verdant east-draining valleys, with their woods and fields and old, stone settlements. This is, indeed, my part of the Pennines, for I have always lived within sight of the deep blue crests of Eastmoor, notably within sight of Totley Moor, Black Hill and Bole Hill, with Brown Edge and Flask Edge rising to the 1,296-foot-high triangulation station under summer sunset and purple on hazy autumn afternoons. The country under the western flanks is short and steep, straight-down-to-the-river country of bracken slopes and gritstone millstones and walled fields, a highway or two climbing out of the valley, then the tree-embowered River Derwent. It is only a very short distance from the top of Eastmoor to the bottom of the Derwent Valley but a different matter if one descends eastwards towards the coalfield country. The dip slope eases away for many miles, and the views out over those wood-and-field sweeps can be truly spectacular in a pastoral and typically English way. The head waters of those streams which help to swell the Ouse and the Humber wind down, at first wild, moorland torrents and then silent curves of shining water by trees and high banks. Take, for instance, the Ewden Beck, as it drains the high cotton-grass mosses known as Upper Commons, which rise to 1,793 feet at Margery Hill on the watershed in the true Black Peak. For a mile or two the stream is a wild child of the Pennine sky as it cuts its brown way through the peat groughs, joining Stainery Clough and so, at 850 feet, entering the contrasting world of deciduous trees in the deepening valley and so by the ancient site of Wigtwizzle above the twin reservoirs below Ewden village, with its Youth Hostel of twenty-four beds. Soon after leaving the lower Ewden Reservoir, the Ewden Beck confludes with the mother-stream, the River Don, on her way down from the source on Grains Moss upon the West Riding-Cheshire boundary.

The Barlow Brook has a much longer course and runs through country far more pastoral throughout. Its source upon the edge of Ramsley Moor is not so lonely as that of the Ewden Beck, though in winter the snow can drift across Leash Fen and cause the knoll-top shepherd's cottage on Ramsley Moor—Ramsley Lodge—to

The main street, Barley, Lancashire

look as if it were at the edge of the world. Soon, though, the
brook falls into coal measure terrain, and the great bulk of conifer-
clad Smeekley Wood (originally the Smooth Cliff) frowns down
and encloses the wooded reaches at the head of Cordwell Valley.
There is no lovelier dale in the Pennines, north, central or south.
Look out from the Sheffield-Baslow main road above Greaves's
Piece on a bright, midsummer evening and see a dozen woodlands, a thousand old, stone farms and the patchwork of field
patterns and sunken lanes appearing as coloured pebbles beneath
the shimmering surface of a clear pool. This is a view in the true
Housman tradition, a view that can cause a pain in the heart.

Living at Ramsley Lodge are Mr. and Mrs. R. B. Bramwell,
who came from Edale some years ago. Mr. Bramwell is the
shepherd for the North Derbyshire Water Board and is one of a
disappearing race of Pennine shepherds, a craftsman who is as
much a part of his hills as the sheep in his care. Their welfare is his
heartfelt concern, and no trouble is too much to overcome in
winter cold or summer heat. In early summer Ramsley Moor
comes alive as we stride through the wind-stunted silver birches
looking for birds' nests and listen to the call of the cuckoo and the
wheatear, newly arrived. From the door of the Lodge looking
eastwards, the stone pillar of Godfrey's Cross is visible less than a
mile away, and that reminds me that this part of Eastmoor is
steeped in history because the ridge had inevitably to be crossed by
travellers journeying between east and west across the main grain
of routes which ran from north to south. Travellers in general and
monks, donkey trains carrying lead and limestone and coal, and
farmers driving animals to market made up the bulk of the heavy
traffic over these heights. A lifetime can be spent in tracing the
remains of the route-ways hereabouts, most of them incon-
spicuous beneath the heather and grassland, with stone markers
the only obvious features left to us.

The most notable remains are the many stone circles near the
Bar Brook and the recently-found cup-and-ring marked stones
upon Big Moor, and Hob Hurst's House beneath Harland Edge
(actually a tumulus). However, there are numerous stones of
lesser antiquity dotting the length of Eastmoor, notably that part

Keighley from the Haworth Road

of it within a rectangle with Fox House Inn at the north-west corner, Owler Bar in the north-east, Darley Hillside at the south-west corner and Holymoorside in the south-east. The average altitude of this rectangle is 1,000 feet, rising to 1,203 feet at White Edge and Harland Edge.

There is a very worn stump of stone at the northern end of Big Moor known as Lady's Cross. It is, no doubt, an old marker stone for a route across this wild moorland, as so many 'crosses' here-abouts have been proved to be. The pack-horse tracks wandered across Eastmoor between Sheffield and Chesterfield to the east and the farmlands of the Peak District to the west.

There is a similar standing 'cross' above the Bar Brook, actually quite close to the 'Swine Sty' shown on the 1-inch Ordnance Survey map. This indicates the destinations on its sides, as does another marker in even better condition by the path from the Chesterfield-Curbar road to Wellington's Monument by the escarpment overlooking the Baslow-Sheffield main road. This latter marker clearly indicates the way to Chesterfield and Baslow and proves that this was the original route down into Baslow, before the modern road in the valley below was made.

Only half-a-mile away, up the Bar Brook, is a very fine slab bridge which carried this route over the water. Today few people see the bridge from the main road and even fewer walk the short distance down to it. On its southern side is the clearly cut date '1777', presumably the year in which this structure replaced an older one.

The late G. H. B. Ward did much research into old trackways and rights of way in this area and was one of the first to point out that such relatively well known 'crosses' as Godfrey's Cross by Fox Lane were sited in conspicuous places to facilitate easy route-finding in bad weather conditions. The last-mentioned stone pillar is now badly weathered but is especially interesting since on one side are carved the words "Here lies Godfrey". Though erosion has made this lettering difficult to see people used to imagine the stone marked the grave of a brave soul lost on the heights—but not so! Godfrey Silcock lived in a cottage down Fox Lane and carved the letters on this stone before emigrating to New Zealand in 1893.

The carving is not so old as often imagined. Across Fox Lane from Godfrey's Cross is what I think is a finer monument to ancient route-marking, a taller cross set in a similar stone socket but now hidden from view by the young conifers of Shillito Plantation.

Who erected these markers? And when? The fact that they are crosses gives a clue. It is probable that they were placed in these wild situations by monks engaged in charitable works in the Middle Ages. These Eastmoor crosses were very likely erected by the monks of Beauchief Abbey.

Another cross stands 1½ miles to the south across the wastes of Leash Fen, close by Clod Hall Lane. This is called Whibbersley Cross and probably marked the line of road which crossed the moor much as the modern lane does, from Chesterfield towards the Derwent Valley. Just across the lane here is the post-Enclosures Act farm of Clod Hall. It was so named, apparently, because of the rough appearance of the first dwelling erected there by a squatter from Robin Hood (near Baslow) called William Kay. In a way the use of the term 'hall' gives a clue to the north Derbyshire countryman's ironic humour, which is still evident a century and a half later.

Before passing farther to the east, mention must be made of the well-known gritstone tors close to Nelson's Monument on Birchen Edge above Robin Hood. Here three large outcrops of millstone grit stand upon the moor-top like ships at sea, and soon after the Battle of Trafalgar they were carved with the names of three of the mightiest ships of the British fleet at that time— *Victory*, *Dreadnought* and *Indefatigable*. The trio and the gaunt column commemorating Nelson look out to the south-west, over the Derwent Valley and lovely Chatsworth Park, only a mile away.

Just over two miles to the east of Birchen Edge is the 980-foot-high summit of Grange Hill, a smooth-sloped eminence overlooking the quilted lands of Barlow Vale and the Linacre Valley. Not far from the road over the hill-top are two short stone pillars, with "Brampton 4" carved upon the sides facing the blunt spire of Old Brampton Church, 4 miles to the south-east. These are parish boundary markers at the perimeter of Old Brampton parish.

They stand in different fields, pointing to the fact that their positions upon the boundary are accurate and not haphazardly placed by the roadside, where they might have been more conveniently erected.

Many have been the long-distance walks completed over these eastern heights, notably the Colne-Rowsley—its 70-mile length ending in the latter village, where the Manchester-bound train could be caught for the return to Lancashire before this main railway route was closed to traffic in 1968. Another is the Dunford Bridge-Rowsley, again convenient as the electrified line took one to Dunford Bridge and the Manchester-bound train took one home from Rowsley. These were walks particularly popular with members of the Manchester-based Rucksack Club. A longer route than the last-mentioned is Dunford Bridge-Crich, 40 miles down the crest of Eastmoor and ending appropriately at the top of the 'last Pennine hill' before the sweep down into Midland nonentity. I don't know of anyone who has completed this route, so I must here describe my own recent experiences when I did the walk on a fine June day and was helped by friends.

An early start is essential for the walk to be completed without the problem of failing light in the latter stages, unless one is keen on night-walking. Early summer is usually the best season for long-distance upland walking, because the days are long and the weather normally reliable. I would advise anyone interested in doing the Dunford Bridge-Crich route to do it from north to south, for then the hardest and most difficult ground is covered first, when one is fresh. There is nothing worse than facing increasingly difficult terrain as one gets tired towards the day's end. Besides, failing light or deteriorating weather is best dealt with south of Beeley Moor and not (unless one is very experienced with map and compass and know the details of the high moorlands to be traversed) high on the Howden Moors or Outer Edge.

After a week of heavy rain I left Dunford Bridge at 5 a.m. on a dark, mist-hung Saturday morning—the last in June. My friends Melvin Campbell and Doug Hanbidge had driven me to this starting point and were to meet me *en route* during the day and finally collect me at Crich Hill. As I left them and ascended up the little valley, which holds two small reservoirs, the first curlews were calling from vague moorland expanses, and soon I was wet to the knees as the rise to Fiddlers Green passed. The vibrations of a goods train on the electrified Woodhead line behind me were soon drowned by the throbbing of heavy lorries going over the trunk road between the Flouch Inn and Longdendale. After crossing this busy road, the long, wild section over Langsett Moor, Howden Moor and Derwent Edge (about 10½ miles) faces one, and in the prevailing conditions I knew that my pace was going to be slowed. Low mist clung to the tops of the ridges separating the various head-streams of the Porter River (the Little Don), but as I dropped steeply into the second transverse clough—Laund Clough—bright carpets of bracken were visible on the opposite bank and were in refreshing contrast to the yellow cloud and grey-brown moor, which suggested its presence in every direction until completely swallowed up by the damp swirls of silent vapour. Silent, that is, save for the regular calls of moor-nesting birds. Grouse calls echoed over all, and here and there a curlew piped its voice from an unseen stance by an imagined bog, where the peaty waters drained and stood after the heavy rains of an unsettled week just gone. An occasional dunlin called, and lapwings cheeped angrily overhead—I must be near their eggs or chicks on these occasions.

Glad of the compass, I walked on southwards, gradually ascending to the watershed. Unfortunately it is a broad and gentle water-parting, the ridge between the Don and the Derbyshire Derwent. Eventually the land ahead eased, and I got the suggestion that the gradient was reversing, the sign for me to turn to the south-east and so make for the top of Outer Edge with its trigonometrical point. In clear weather the exercise is a simple one if you know the terrain, and one can take the shortest route by making for the silhouettes of the topmost rocks on Outer Edge. In the prevailing conditions that wasn't possible and I had to hope that my map and compass navigation was reasonably accurate. For some time I floundered in ankle-deep bog and found myself too far down on the Derwent side of the ridge, but by 6.30 a.m. I had covered the 4½ miles from Dunford Bridge to Outer Edge, ten minutes longer than on a previous occasion, when visibility had been good and the underfoot going much better.

To the south the long, broad ridge continues for many miles over several summits where gritstone tors lie outcropped above the general level of the moor. The next top is the highest point of the whole route and is called Margery Hill (1,793 feet), a broad summit-rise of peat and heather and indefinite shapes so that I expected difficulty in locating the summit. After wandering off to the east and finding it necessary to ascend up the head-reaches of Bull Clough, the ancient trackway crossing from Penistone into Derwent Dale, called Cut Gate, was located so that I was able to follow to the indefinite crest of the watershed again, then south-wards over Margery Hill, and so by Featherbed Moss into the great trench of the Abbey Brook, where the Peakland moors probably reach their most dramatic contour shapes. Here is a great, winding trough worn out by the Abbey Brook from the gritstones and shales; here and there is evidence of landslips, and there are several vertical exposures of instable gritstone and shales. Up on the southern side I passed the now ruinous Abbey Brook shooting cabins, which have been reduced to splintered wood and rubble in the past decade by the influx of vandals and so-called ramblers. The crossing of the upper end of the Abbey Clough has entailed a descent and ascent of almost 700 feet from the crest level, but once the great outcrop of gritstone marking the summit of Back Tor (1,765 feet) has been gained there is a relatively level track southwards, and I put the map and compass into the rucksack. The West Riding-Derbyshire boundary runs up from the mouth of Abbey Brook in Derwent Dale to Back Tor's summit and from here one stays inside Derbyshire—with the exception of a mile to the south of Stanage Edge—for the rest of the journey to Crich. The time was 8 a.m., and, despite the delay caused by wet going and the low cloud, I had done these first nine miles in less than three hours.

The very top of Back Tor was covered by cloud, but the worn track kept me to the escarpment's broad crest, and very soon I was passing the humorous group of tors called the Cakes of Bread. Up on to the 1,656-foot-top of Dovestone Tor with its fine view when this thick mist doesn't interrupt. This vantage point was known as early as 1571 as Doweston Torr—perhaps Dowerstone Tor or Rock? On again, with a glimpse of the conspicuous Salt Cellar, which is one of the finest shaped upstanding gritstone pillars of the Pennines. Then White Tor and the Coach and Horses (or the Wheel Stones), grouped in array on the broad part of Derwent Edge. In a little over half a mile the Hurkling Stones come up. These were referred to by this name in 1823, as evidenced by plans in the Fairbank Collection in Sheffield Public Library, and it is probably a derivation of Urconedge Hill which appeared on several old maps of the district, including that by C. Saxton in 1577 and the one by J. Speed in 1610.

In less than a mile one has descended gently over bracken and heather, then through deciduous trees, to the Sheffield-Glossop road a short distance above the Ladybower Inn. Melvin and Doug were waiting for me when I arrived at 8.30 a.m. The $12\frac{1}{4}$ miles so far covered constitute the roughest part of the journey, and at 9.10 a.m. I set out up wooded Jarvis Clough, making for the northern end of Stanage Edge. Actually the best route over the boggy terrain at the head of Jarvis Clough is to make for a line of shooting butts and so up to High Neb, the highest point on Stanage Edge. Here the West Riding-Derbyshire boundary reaches the very crest for a short distance before slipping off to the south-east across the Hallam Moors.

Stanage Edge always takes me longer to cross from north to south than I anticipate, and on this particular morning it seemed to reach out endlessly into the thinning cloud. Suddenly the sun was shining vaguely and the air grew warm. Already there were parties of climbers on the Edge or scrambling up through the bracken at its foot.

By 10.40 a.m. I was on the top of Higger Tor and back in the West Riding again. On over Carl Wark, the flat-topped Iron Age hill-fort with massive dry-stone walling still rising to over nine feet in height, and down to the Hathersage-Sheffield road a short distance below Fox House Inn, where the green estate car came into sight beyond boulders, bracken and heather. After refreshments with Melvin and Doug I set off through the grounds of Longshaw Lodge, once a shooting lodge belonging to the Dukes of Rutland. It was built about 1830 but has been much enlarged since that date. The walk was made all the finer because the plentiful rhododendrons were in full bloom and in sharp contrast to the mist-covered miles behind. In 3 miles I was passing the Grouse Inn, and soon the 2½-mile section along the dry and rocky crest of Froggatt Edge and Curbar Edge was begun. A storm was now threatening from behind, from the north. I quickened my pace and by 12.25 p.m. had gained Curbar Gap, the low point in this part of the Eastmoor escarpment, where the old road from Chesterfield and Old Brampton to Manchester goes and nowadays attracts so many motorists to park their cars on fine weekends. Over 22½ miles had now been completed, and the storm threats from behind seemed to have passed away. Nearby, upon the highest part of Curbar Edge, my old friend E. Hector Kyme spent a difficult June evening trying to obtain suitable photographs for this book before the western sun became obscured behind advancing clouds.

A mile of road walking followed, and then I took to the moor again, aiming for the foot of Birchen Edge, where the Three Battleship rocks and Nelson's Monument stand. There were climbers here too, and, as the sun came out to give me fresh energy, I went down through the bracken to Robin Hood, a hamlet of a house, an inn and an ivy-clad farmhouse upon the Chesterfield-Baslow road. And here, in the sunshine, the weekend traffic roared, families couped up in the stuffy depth of their cars and coaches belching lethal diesel fumes. Within minutes I had dropped from the roadside, crossed the Umberley Brook and entered Chatsworth territory. How glad I was to be on foot and not a willing captive upon that busy road. It was now 1.30 p.m., and my route lay round the edge of coniferous woodland and so on to the top of Bunker's Hill above Chatsworth's famous lakes, which supply water to the pleasure gardens far below. Actually it is the planted wood clothing the western slopes of the escarpment here which is called Bunker's Hill Wood, not a wood growing on

Bunker's Hill. The wood is named in memory of the Battle of Bunker's Hill on the outskirts of Boston, Massachusetts, which took place on 17th June 1775 and constituted the first encounter in the American Civil War, when the English stormed the hill which was being fortified by the Americans.

Soon I crossed the stony waste marking the route of the gas pipe leading from the Thames northwards into Yorkshire. One can follow its broad progress right up the length of Eastmoor, largely on the dip slope, but slowly Nature is healing the wounds. Below I could see the ruins of Hob Hurst's House among the lengthening bracken, and then it was away over the indefinite crest of little Harland Edge and through knee-deep bracken until the green estate car came into view at Beeley Moor cross-roads. It was 2.40 p.m., and 28½ miles of the walk were behind me. The rest would be easy for it followed lanes and there was little variation in vertical height.

Away to the south-west the 'cardboard castle' outline of Smedley's ridiculous Riber Castle came into view, now doing good service as a Fauna Reserve, where many species of wild creatures from these islands and the Continent are kept and encouraged to breed, in the hope that increasing numbers will eventually enable some to be set free in the wild. The long, ridge-top lane leads the walker southwards by the Wire Stone at 1,044 feet above sea-level, and so to the top of Amber Hill, where the road winds steeply up from Chesterfield and the nearby Amber Valley *en route* for Matlock on the western side. I ran the next pleasant half-mile for a change, with the sun breaking through and the country all about me slipping by. After the shelter of the coniferous woodland at Dethick Common, where rhododendrons and blackbirds made another happy change, the lane winds on towards the thirty-sixth mile above the little-known village of Wheatcroft, and now Crich Stand was clear ahead, the end of a memorable day was now coming close.

By Plaistow and Plaistow Green I went, between dark hedges and dark, stone walls. In a roadside field a man attended to the feet of a lame hunter, and a jay flew in flashing-winged splendour into a copse of ash trees. The land was falling away nicely now, the open land of Midland country was suggested ahead beyond the roof-tops of Crich and the sharp spire of St. Michael's parish church. A corner turned brought the iron gates leading to the Stand into sight, and as I walked up to the top of the hill that tenacious green estate car drew in behind me and Melvin and Doug climbed out and followed me to the top.

Crich Stand was erected in the inter-war years as a memorial to the 11,409 men of the Sherwood Foresters Regiment who fell in World War I. Every night a bright searchlight sweeps the Derbyshire sky from the lighthouse-like turret, and on the first Sunday in July each year there is a great pilgrimage to the memorial. I sat upon the trigonometrical point at 939 feet above sea-level and surveyed the world of limestone at my feet, where the disused quarry-face falls Derwent-wards to the west. To the east and south the Pennines slip down as woods and fields to the Midland Plain.

Behind, away under that sky and mingled cloud, the Backbone of England rose in darkening swells. Escarpment shapes and rounded moor-tops, one behind the other, led the eye and mind into infinity. A whole wonder world of upland contrasts lie that way, a world which no one can become fully intimate with in a single lifetime.

CHAPTER XIV

THE PENNINE WAY

THE Pennine Way is *the* modern feature of the whole ridge, modern because it is a comparatively recent innovation which has little to do with the age-old activities of this hill country. It has developed because of the needs of urban development—I think it true to say that had we remained a largely rural and agri-cultural people few would wish to undertake long-distance walks on the hills, for a rest (or change) would have really meant a rest, change from outdoor activity or work. The long-distance foot-path along the Pennines ridge measures more than the stated 250 miles and is, in fact, about 270 miles in length. It starts in the south at Edale, at the heart of the Black Peak, and ends at Kirk Yetholm among the Cheviots—beyond Pennine country—just over the Scottish border. You will notice that I say "starts at Edale"; most walkers of the notable 270 miles start in the south, though there is no valid argument against doing it in the reverse direction except, maybe, that the opening-up of the route as one progresses north-wards is more rewarding and the changes in scenery more logical. Perhaps some walkers would be put off a north-south journey by the comparatively stiff going of the last thirty or so miles over the peaty levels of Black Hill, Bleaklow and Kinder Scout, though I would consider such a final interesting challenge, in fine weather, a most rewarding finale.

The names of Tom Stephenson and the Pennine Way are synonymous, for this notable rambler and champion of access to open country was born in 1893 in Lancashire, within sight of the western Pennines, and developed a deep affection for these northern hills from an early age. Lack of money did not deter

young Tom, and when short of work in the years of unemploy-
ment in Lancashire between 1907 and 1912 he took more and
more to the hills, often undertaking walks of thirty or more miles.
Journalism became Tom Stephenson's career in 1933 when he
joined the staff of the *Daily Herald* as the paper's open-air corre-
spondent, and subsequently his "Afoot in Britain" series of
articles became very popular, helping to stimulate the already-
growing enthusiasm for rambling and the countryside. The
Pennine Way was born by accident in 1935, for two American
girls who were keen ramblers wrote to the *Daily Herald* asking for
details of a walking route right up the high ground marking the
watershed of northern England. Tom Stephenson planned the
route for them, and this set him thinking along the lines of a public
footpath stretching the length of the Pennines so that any interested
rambler could follow in these girls' footsteps. Three years later he
formed the Pennine Way Association, but many more years were
to pass before the numerous problems related to access and rights-
of-way were reduced to a mere handful. By 1964 the last right-
of-way to be disputed was considered at a public inquiry. The
point at issue was the line of the route in Upper Redesdale,
Northumberland. The Northern Area of the Ramblers' Association, represented by Tom Stephenson, wanted—and still want—
the route to keep to high, open country north of the summit of
Brownrigg Head, making for Blackwool Law about half a mile
distant then descending to the River Rede close by the Edinburgh-
Newcastle road (A68) to start the final twenty-nine miles of high,
Cheviot country to the northern terminus at Kirk Yetholm.
Though the inspector decided in favour of the Ramblers' Association proposals, the Ministry of Housing and Local Government
rejected his recommendations and placed the route down to
Rookengate from the top of Brownrigg Head and thence
through the dense Redesdale Forest until the river is gained;
altogether a less satisfactory way for the Pennine walker, as it
keeps one off the open ridge-top at an important place, where the
last hard section towards Kirk Yetholm may be viewed in clear
conditions.

The route was now complete, and any hardy rambler could

cover the 270 miles on public rights-of-way. At a most impressive ceremony on Malham Moor the Pennine Way was opened officially on 24th April 1965. A great gathering of walkers and mountaineers listened to Lord Strong, Chairman of the National Parks Commission, and to the Right Honourable F. Wiley, Minister of Land and Natural Resources. The originator of the route addressed the crowd too—it was a happy occasion and good to hear Tom Stephenson recounting the problems overcome.

There are four outstanding books describing the Pennine Way, and the rambler intending to follow the route will find them invaluable. Anyone, in fact, who is interested in this large upland area will do well to have these volumes. Firstly, there is that classic book of photographs called *The Backbone of England* by W. A. Poucher, F.R.P.S. It was published by *Country Life* in 1946 and is now, unfortunately, out of print, though still obtainable from public libraries. Here is a feast for the eyes; large plates of hills, dales and pot-holes, moorland, village and fine skyscapes. It is one of my favourite books of photographs.

The second book is by my friend Kenneth Oldham and is simply called *The Pennine Way*. Published by the Dalesman Publishing Company in 1960, it describes the route from Edale to Kirk Yetholm, largely by means of an account of the author's experiences with parties of young people—in fact, he led the first school party along the full-length of the Way. It makes interesting reading and is especially useful as background material to familiarize oneself with the country to be crossed.

The next book is again by Poucher and is a straightforward guide to the various sections of Pennine country. It is called *The Peak and Pennines*, published by Constable in 1966, and is packed with useful photographs (many with the described routes over-marked upon them). Like Kenneth Oldham's *The Pennine Way*, this one is suitable for the pocket or rucksack and would, I know, prove invaluable to any Pennine or Peakland rambler.

The last of the notable quartet is also the most recent book. It is a real gem from the pen of that famous Lakelander, A. Wainwright. In this pocket-book, entitled *Pennine Way Companion*, the author shows again his unequalled skill with words and sketches. Every page is printed from photographed reproductions of the author's original manuscript, each one a work of art. The entire route, every wall and stile and boggy place, each noteworthy object and distant view is recorded so that the walker neither loses his way or his interest. The pen and ink sketches are very fine and certainly represent many hours of careful observation and detailed execution. This one volume, published in 1968 by the *Westmorland Gazette*, is enough to carry along the length of the route, as it certainly keeps you to "the straight and narrow" and, as a bonus, makes for pleasant and amusing leisure evening reading while planning the next day's section.

The problem facing the walker on the Pennine Way is overnight accommodation along it. Keeping largely to high and uninhabited territory the Way is best suited to the lightweight camper, who is free to stop virtually where the fancy pleases, though camping sites are sometimes difficult to locate in the few sections of lowland traversed. With a few exceptions it is necessary to leave the actual route and descend to east or west for the night; one exception being Ponden Hall near Haworth (already mentioned in an earlier chapter), which lies right beside the path and offers refreshments and accommodation to travellers.

Another problem is Pennine weather—August is often cloudy and wet—and for that reason I would suggest that the best times are April-May and September-October, when settled conditions are common. June is often a good month, though it can be very hot if clear skies dominate in midsummer. A period of anticyclonic weather in January-February may well appeal to the experienced rambler, though a shortage of daylight would necessitate much night walking or a protracted holiday to cover the mileage. A normal walking time is two weeks or fifteen days, but it is possible to complete the route in less time, though I do not know of anyone doing it in ten days or less. Such times would of necessity turn a revealing and pleasant journey into a gruelling marathon with little point save the vigorous exercise involved.

It is the contrasts in scenery and in types of walking that make the Way so rewarding. Think, for a moment, of those contrasts—

the high, open heights of millstone-grit country northwards from
Edale, which includes the most difficult territory of all as far as
Thornton; the pleasant limestone country of Craven between
Thornton and Penyghent; the wilder country again of Dodd Fell,
Upper Wensleydale, Great Shunner Fell, upper Swaledale and Tan
Hill; there is equally wild country beyond too, but of a different
character in Teesdale and over Cross Fell to Alston and the Roman
Wall; then comes difference again, the hills and villages which
lead to the great forests and rolling shoulders of Cheviot country,
which are quite different from anything which has gone before.

By planning wisely, any strong walker will enjoy his days up
(or down) the 'backbone' of northern England, with lightweight
tent or reliance on strategically placed Youth Hostels and/or
guest houses. Only the weather remains relatively unpredictable,
but the Pennines are enjoyable in rain and wind as well as when
the sun shines from a cloudless sky.

CHAPTER XV

THE SHEEP OF PEAKLAND

OVER hundreds of years the sheep farmers of these islands have developed breeds of sheep best suited to local conditions. The Cotswold evolved as a large animal at home on the porous limestone pasture-land of the Cotswold Hills, the Blackface on the high rainfall uplands of the Pennines and later as the Scottish Blackface in western Scotland, and so on. In the Pennines a number of breeds took shape, all of them belonging to the group known as Mountain or Hill Breeds. In the northern Pennines the very hardy Rough Fell and the smaller Swaledale, the Teeswater and the large-bodied Wensleydale came into being, and these breeds, together with the Blackface dominate the hill grazings and open moorland.

The same pattern developed in the southern Pennines, too. In the Peak District a number of local breeds were developed, some of them very local in distribution, and with the present-day tendency to standardize farm animals, as with most other things which have formerly lent variety and character to life, some of them have become virtually extinct. One of the pleasures of rambling over the gritstone moorlands is to notice the different types of sheep living thereon.

The Lonk is a relatively large animal and is characterized by having plenty of white upon its face. In recent years it has been displaced to some extent by the Scottish Blackface, because the latter is better able to withstand heavy snowfall. The Lonk was developed in the central Pennines, especially in eastern Lancashire, where its fine, dense and heavy fleece is excellent protection against prolonged, heavy rain. Over the years the Lonk became

Main Street, Haworth

more popular with sheep farmers in Peakland, and the characteristic long, swinging tail helped to identify it as it trotted off
across the heather and peat. This breed is still seen in north-
western Peakland, over in Cheshire and south-eastern Lancashire,
and its wool is best used for blanket manufacture.

The Dale o' Goyt was a breed developed, not surprisingly, in
the Goyt Valley of western Derbyshire. The River Goyt rises on
Goyt's Moss very close to the Cat and Fiddle Inn, second highest
public house in England. Many people classify the infant Goyt as
the true source of the River Mersey, and it certainly has a claim to
that honour. A century ago the Dale o' Goyt, with its speckled
black-and-grey face, was important, and in time it spread throughout the sheepwalks of Peakland, becoming known as the Derbyshire Gritstone. It is a larger breed than the Blackface, has face and
legs dark with white markings, is hornless and possesses a fine,
soft fleece. This is the best known of all Peakland breeds, but
today it has lost ground to the Blackface, and there are only a
handful of pure-bred Derbyshire Gritstone flocks left, notably in
the valley of their origin. At Fernilee Hall Farm lives J. J. Brocklehurst, whose Derbyshire Gritstones have carried off many
championships, both for first-class animals and quality fleeces.
Indeed, the Brocklehurst family, who farm throughout the Goyt
Valley, dominate the world of this particular breed. Wander over
the moorland above the two Goyt Valley Reservoirs—Fernilee
and the newly-constructed Errwood—and the chances are that
the sheep seen will be Derbyshire Gritstones.

Not so easily seen, in fact virtually extinct except as types, are
two other local breeds. One is the Penistone, which originated as a
typical Pennine breed in the upland around the market town of
that name on the very northern borders of the Peak District. It
became unpopular in the face of competition from the Blackface,
as did the other breed—the Limestone—which was once kept in
quite considerable flocks on and near the porous limestone
plateau of central and western Derbyshire.

Of all local breeds, though, maybe the most romantic from an
historical point of view is the White-faced Woodland. It has

9

received very little attention in textbooks and deserves careful consideration for its story is the story of the evolution of Peakland sheep farming.

When John Farey reported in his *Survey of the Agriculture of Derbyshire*, published between 1811 and 1817, that eighty farmers had White-faced Woodland flocks in the north-west corner of that county, most of the wool from these sheep was sold for "the hatter's use", though the "long tails of rams are sheared for carpet making". The White-faced Woodland breed of sheep is of very ancient origin. It was very popular in medieval times in the uplands of the Peak District, and flocks numbering hundreds formerly roamed the remote wilderness of heather moor, for it was one of only four breeds kept in the county. They were large, heavy sheep with good wool and plain, grey faces. Both sexes are horned. Due to the decline in the demand for large joints, the breed lost favour over the years so there was only one breeder left by 1939.

In recent decades the breed was used for crossing with Swaledale ewes to increase and retain size in that smaller breed. This crossing has inevitably led to some loss of the true character of the breed. However, today there are three or four Peak District sheep farmers who take an active interest in the breed, and, thanks to them, the White-faced Woodland has not become extinct.

On a recent spring afternoon I arrived at Lady Booth Farm, Edale, the home of the Shirt family. Here a few of these old-fashioned sheep are kept. I looked out of the big windows of the house, through the branches of a sycamore, to the steep, sunny slopes of Back Tor across the valley. Mrs. Shirt, now 80 years old, recalled for me the days when there were flocks consisting of hundreds of White-faced Woodland sheep. She showed me an old photograph taken on her uncle's farm at Hayfield, on the far side of Kinder Scout (2,088 feet), depicting a large flock held in the corner of a field for the half-plate camera.

"Those sheep were far larger, plainer animals than they are now; big joints were wanted then," Mrs. Shirt recalled. "They are fine milkers but never did very well on lowland farms," she added.

This last fact was substantiated by a remark made by John Farey a century-and-a-half ago, when he wrote that great loss and inconvenience was often experienced when the sheep were over-wintered in lowland areas, the animals "being very badly kept and treated, and taking the rot (footrot) when thus removed from their owner's inspection during the worst half of the year".

Mrs. Shirt possesses a copy of *The Orders of the Shepherd's Society now held at the House of Joseph Brocklehurst, in Hayfield*. This was first published in 1790, and the copy I saw was dated 1803. It was a meeting of "the principal Sheep Keepers in the liberties of Woodland, Edale, Hayfield and Glossop". Each flockmaster had his peculiar horn-mark, and this was noted in this booklet for identification purposes, and so that no farmer "should be guilty of ignorance of a sheep's ownership".

The Shirts' farm is 380 acres of in-by land (land adjacent to uncultivated moorland which is fenced and more akin to the lower, cultivated fields than to the wild hill grazings) in the Vale of Edale, plus about 1,000 acres of 'gated' land on Kinder Scout owned by the National Trust—wild moorland approaching the 2,000-feet contour, where an agreed number of sheep are allowed to graze each year.

Another authority on the breed was the late Frank Greaves of Offerton Hall Farm, near Hathersage. The Greaves were factors for the Dukes of Devonshire at Rowlee Farm in the Hope Woodlands for three centuries. Charles Greaves had two flocks of White-faced Woodland sheep at Rowlee at the beginning of the last century when he was the factor there.

In this connection, Mr. L. M. Waud, the County Agricultural Officer for Derbyshire, believes that it was the Duke of Devonshire of that time who was responsible for the introduction of fresh blood into the stock, which had remained unaltered for so many centuries. He brought Merino rams to serve the Woodlands flocks, to improve the quantity and quality of his tenant's wool harvest.

At Crookhill Farm, Ashopton, on the hills overlooking Ladybower Reservoir below the Hope Woodlands, Mr. Eric Elliott

maintains what is perhaps the largest flock of White-faced Woodlands, a relic breed of these wild uplands that has largely lost its
economic importance but without which the Peak District would
be the duller and the poorer.

CHAPTER XVI

LIFE ON A PENNINE FARM

A MISCONCEPTION was abroad in the years following World War II that many farmers had a relatively easy life, with big incomes swelled by generous Government subsidies. Needless to say, that was an almost exclusively urban view and one which was largely erroneous. Many hill farmers received fairly large subsidies for their breeding cattle, calves and sheep, but such income was essential on most upland holdings, where high rainfall, long winters and poor-quality land produces small returns on capital investment.

Hill farming in the Pennines is usually a hard life, but there are several facets to it which give it advantages when compared with lowland farming patterns. Many large upland holdings do not have a dairy herd, and the work can, therefore, be termed spasmodic—weeks of continuous toil punctuated by periods when there is less to do. In this way the hill farmer can often take time off for a break when his lowland counterpart must be back for afternoon milking. I recall a mountain farmer reminding me of that feature of his life some years ago; he explained it very well. "When the dipping is over, I can, you see, go off to the coast for three or four days with an easy mind, for there is no corn to ripen and harvest, and the cows are milked by their own calves!"

That is not to say, of course, that hill farming is easy—besides, the majority of Pennine holdings produce milk for sale anyway, so the above argument does not apply. Only on the larger (usually mountain) farms, where sheep and beef cattle are the main sources of income, does hill farming come into its own and sometimes overbalance the scales against the lowland dairy or mixed holding.

But what is life on the hill really like? I can speak from experience on several hill farms, but one of them will have to suffice here.

It stands in millstone grit country at 750 feet above sea-level and half-way down a north-west facing clough, backed by high brown hills and a plateau which exceeds 2,000 feet. The land extends to almost 1,000 acres. Though the farmhouse and buildings face the north, the sheltering hills behind, which rise up suddenly on two sides, give the place a less bleak appearance, an appearance which is upheld in practice when strong winds blow in from the west, for the farm is relatively favoured—only a north wind manages to make the situation really inhospitable. Then the blasts are funnelled up the clough and buffet the buildings fearfully.

Built about two centuries ago, the house is probably an improvement on an older dwelling for the rest of the buildings are certainly older and suggest the site of a farm over a much longer period. The house is four-square and typically Pennine; a central front door and windows either side. The door leads out into the farmyard, cobbled and rough but kept cleaner than many I know. The door at the back of the house opens into a passage under the hill, and the stone flags here are always green with moss. Ferns grow out of the wall, which keeps the hill-side in its place and on to which the windows at the back of the house look out. The buildings are typical of a big-acreage northern hill farm—large stone barn with high-arched doorway along its length so that loads of hay could be brought inside and unloaded more easily in the days when the scythe (later the mowing machine) and hay-forks were the implements used on the nearby in-by land. If bad weather threatened, maybe a storm, a load could be backed into the barn under that high-arched door by the horses and left in safety until there was time to throw it off. Small doors high up on either side of the doorway are called 'picking holes', and as the hay filled the barn the last loads were thrown up through them and passed into the hot and gloomy depths under the stone-slated roof.

The other buildings form two sides of a square, the farmhouse filling part of the third side, and the fourth side, to the east, lies open and just above the gurgling beck, which rushes in most seasons down the bed of the clough in the early stages of its journey to the Irish Sea. There is a cowshed, more properly called a cow-byre in this district, for half a dozen cattle, and there are several loose boxes. The stable has long been used as a food store because the last draught horse left the farm soon after the last war, replaced by the ubiquitous little grey tractor which was Harry Ferguson's brain-child and which became such a boon to the majority of hill farmers in post-war days. With its transporter box attached to the hydraulic arms at the back, it was used here for a score of tasks, from carting hay to sheep in the middle of winter to fetching churns of water for the cattle in times of summer drought. The tractor was also used before the Land-Rover came for taking the women along the rough lane to catch the bus down into the town. And in deep snows it took them all the way to the town centre and back. But the Land Rover makes the journey more quickly and, with its four-wheel drive, can get through in almost any conditions. Those two vehicles have revolutionized hill farmers' lives more than the coming of calor gas or electricity for it has made possible the undertaking and completion of more in the day than would have been dreamed of in pre-war days—even if hill farmers get less exercise as a direct result. To cart hay to the sheep took all morning when a light draught horse was used to pull a high-sided cart up to the snow-covered fields higher up the clough; today the tractor pulls the trailer up the track, the hay is scattered for the flock, and the return journey is completed within an hour or so, leaving more time for other winter jobs in the yard.

When I first visited the farm more than fifteen years ago the farmer was an old man but still active. He had been there for most of his working life, and under his careful husbandry the in-by land had been improved, the sheep flock increased in size and quality, and the typical Shorthorn herd had been replaced by Galloways, animals better suited to the severe winters and extensive grazings. He was a tall, lean man with bushy moustache and brown, leathery face and hands.

It was he who explained the basic principle underlying sound dry-stone walling:

One a' top o' two,
Two a' top o' one.

By this method there never occurs that deadliest of dry-stone walling sins, a double joint where two courses end one above the other and so cause looseness and weakness in the wall. One particularly fine wall runs by the old Roman road—now just a rough track—winding up the bed of the clough close to the beck. The topmost course, below the coping stones, is formed of large, wide stones which overhang both sides of the wall and so help to prevent the agile moorland sheep from jumping over. Actually these sheep tend to climb up and over a wall, using the projecting stones which inevitably occur for their hooves to gain a purchase; the overhang of a few inches near the top tends to deter them. The typical Wensleydale wall has two or three courses of projecting stones, and though this looks most attractive it can be argued that the lower courses assist the sheep to get a footing in their attempts to scale the obstacle.

The old farmer was an authority on several breeds of moorland sheep which had been economically important in earlier days; and on the farm he was assisted by two sons. Now the old man is dead, and his two sons run the farm as a limited company. Here, where so much of a former age lingers and the ghosts of long-dead shepherds can still be felt in the mossy lee of gritstone tors or on bilberry slopes, is a holding run on modern, productive lines by traditional Pennine skill and industry. Life remains active here, and the ring of children's voices sounds from the cobbled yard across the clough to mingle with the call of lapwings over the pastures and curlews on the moor.

It was decided that the hardy and semi-self-supporting nature of Galloway cattle would make them an ideal breed for the conditions prevailing here, and twenty years ago the first batch of in-calf cows arrived with a bull. Being excellent grazers of rough pastures, they are commonest in their native hills of south-western Scotland (Kirkcudbright and Wigton) but are now popular over the border in Cumberland, and, to a lesser extent, throughout the Pennines. Only the West Highland can compare with the Galloway for ability to withstand—and thrive—in really severe condi-

tions. The herd has been built up over the years, and in spring the
lower fields echo to the calls of woolly calves and their dams.
Most pure-bred Galloways are black, but there are often dun
animals in a herd; here there are quite a number of these mar-
malade cows with similarly coloured calves at foot. I know of no
lovelier calves than these, their chunky, flaxen-coated appearance
belying the wild temperament for which they are known. However, the extent of this wildness varies according to how they are
managed; regular handling does make them more amenable to man.

On this farm a small field with several gateways leading to
adjoining fields has a cattle-crush of galvanized steel tubes set in
one corner. Here a cow can be held while it receives attention—
maybe an injection for an ailment or hoof trimming. Of course,
the spring is the time when the breeding cows are at their wildest,
protecting their new calves against the approach of the farmer or a
dog. At this time, too, the bull is not to be trifled with; he takes a
keen interest in the well-being of the herd as is normal with all
wild or semi-wild cattle. The fact that Galloways are beef animals
and wander over remote country for much of their lives means
that they rarely come to terms with man as do lowland beef or
dairy herds. But the stranger must not think that these are dangerous animals to be avoided at all costs. Even in the spring a
Galloway herd will not take much notice of a passer-by if he does
not attempt to interfere. The worst thing he can do is to wander
with a dog into a herd with calves at foot. The cows will take
exception to such an intrusion, and this breed can then be, quite
understandably, positively dangerous.

Most of the calves born here in the late spring are suckled by
their mother in the lowest-lying pastures and in late summer are
moved to higher ground. Some of the young stock are sold off in
the autumn to lowland farms, where they will be grazed for a
further year or more before slaughter or, in some cases, used for
breeding. Of course, some of the best calves are kept on our
Pennine farm for future breeding, to replace the old cows as they
pass their zenith. Some of these old cattle are sold off to lowland
farms where they can be expected to continue as useful breeding
animals in the more amenable conditions. Occasionally a

particularly sound bull-calf is reared to be sold as a future sire, but most of the male calves will be castrated just before or soon after sale to the lowland farmer. And so the cycle of the hill cattle goes on; the black and dun animals dot the distant summer hillside or shelter behind a wall on a snowy winter day and await the rumble of the tractor with its load of silage and hay as it climbs the Roman track towards them.

The increase in popularity of silage-making in post-war years led to the development of improved methods of conserving this winter feed. Some of these methods proved better than others, and, on hill farms in the north especially, the best conserved silage proved a boon, both when the crop is ensiled and later when the silage is used for winter feeding of the stock. Here, particularly, silage-making has revolutionized a number of facets of work because the threat of summer rain does not unduly hinder progress, while all work inevitably ceases in the hayfields. A long pit has been excavated from a suitable bank near the buildings, and the mowed grass is carted here, compacted by the tractor wheels and eventually sealed with plastic bags. Proteolytic enzymes present in the crop change the protein into amino acids, and fungi and bacteria change the carbohydrates to form various organic acids. These acids prevent other bacteria from ruining the silage, which is preserved for several seasons if necessary. The beauty of this form of conservation here in the Pennines—and in other upland regions—is that the onset of poor weather does not prevent silage-making from continuing, and in a heavy drizzle the tractor continues to cart loads of cut grass from the fields across the clough, along the stony track and round the end of the barn to the pit in the steep slope. When winter comes the pit is opened, and the strong, sweet smell of the silage fills the air over a considerable area as the hay-knife cuts large blocks from the pit. These are thrown loose on to a trailer and taken to the Galloways on the lower slopes of the moor. In very severe winter weather the cattle come down close to the buildings and rely almost entirely upon the carted silage and hay brought to them. At such times, too, the sheep are fed.

Silage has not entirely replaced hay on this farm, of course, but the risks and worry of making hay in a doubtful season are reduced considerably. The hay that is made here compliments nicely the silage, and the variety offered keeps the appetites of the animals keen.

The sheep are not particularly attracted to hand-feeding and will keep alive on the poorest winter herbage until a heavy snow-fall blankets all, and then they will reluctantly turn to the hay put down for them. These hill sheep are the main enterprise on the 900 acres of moorland. Once the flock consisted almost entirely of Lonks and Derbyshire Gritstones, but in the last twenty years there has been an infusion of Blackface blood so that anyone walking over the moors above the clough will see a predominance of ewes and lambs with the characteristic black face and horns.

The Lonks—with black and white face, trim fleece, large horns and long tail—has been kept for centuries in the central Pennines, both in Lancashire and Yorkshire. On this farm hundreds were to be seen in pre-war days because the breed is hardy, nimble of hoof and a good ranger able to find its own food on the poorest heather moors. The Derbyshire Gritstone has never been a really wide-spread breed, and its range has declined as the Blackface has spread. This latter is today the most numerous breed in the British Isles and for good reason. Though we often think of it as originating in Scotland, the truth is that it came also from the northern Pennines, and throughout this watershed of northern England the breed is important nowadays. It is one of the hardiest of hill sheep and can survive on the very poorest vegetation for long periods and in the severest of weathers. After a bad winter on high ground the Blackface ewes will produce a lamb crop of 100 per cent. By the age of four months half the flock of whether (ram) lambs will be fat and be ready for sale to the butcher, and the gimmer (ewe) lambs will be reared to replace the old ewes of the flock or for sale as young breeding ewes later on.

Throughout the Pennines the terms used for different sexes and ages of sheep has created an intricate and complicated pattern which is confusing and misleading. Take, for instance, the tradi-tional terms used for an uncastrated male between its first and second shearing; it can be a Shearing, Shearling or Shear hogg, a Diamond ram, a Dinmont ram or a One-Shear tup. It all depends where the farm is and in what part of the Pennines the sheep farmer was brought up.

The work of the sheep farmer or, rarely nowadays, his shepherd is very much seasonal. Lambing on this farm is kept as late as possible so that the risk of lamb losses from hard weather is reduced. It is usually under way by mid-March, and thereafter the flock is gone round at least once a day to ear-mark and inject the newborn lambs, to help with any ewe in difficulties and to search for foxes or roaming dogs which would undoubtedly kill and injure ewes and lambs. On some large farms of the northern Pennines the shepherd goes on the back of a stocky fell pony, but here the work is done on foot.

Lambing is followed by shearing in early July, a job made easier and quicker by the purchase of electrical shears. When I first visited this farm the hundreds of ewes had to be sheared in the traditional way with hand-clippers, and I well remember the old farmer saying, "After t'first fifty ewes yer 'ands getten used t' job and yer muscles gets firm in t'right places." That was true, and hand shearing really made a first-class job of the animals when done by experts, as this family were. But with the coming of electricity mechanical shears were purchased; now the job is done more quickly, and the finished ewes don't look quite so attractive at the end of the operation.

Dipping of the sheep is now done once only, later in the summer. At one time the sheep were dipped several times for the pesticides used in the dipping water were not so effective as nowadays, and often maggots reinfested the animals. An elaborate system of pens has been devised to reduce the manpower necessary at dipping and other times when the flock has to be handled. The sheep are dipped, and at this time the lambs are separated from the ewes. For some days and nights the hills ring with the calls of ewes and lambs distressed by their mutual loss, but eventually the divided lots settle down and the clough is quiet once again. As the dipping takes place it is normal to count both ewes and lambs and mark their fleece with the particular symbol of the flock so that animals can later be easily identified upon the hill. It was when the old farmer was counting the ewes at a dipping long ago, as they ran timidly through an opening into the field from the pens, that I first heard the local shepherd's numerals. These numerals are traditional and vary from district to district in the British Isles; I am led to believe that they are of very ancient origin and, because some bear a marked similarity to Welsh numerals, it is likely that they originated in Celtic times. Then there is the fact that several are very much like Latin words — maybe they are the result of adulteration, picking up features of various important languages with the passage of time. Anyhow, the numerals once used exclusively on this farm but less often heard today are still remembered. Here are those from one to ten:

Yan, tan, tethera, pethera, pimp, sethera, lethera, hovera, covera, dik.

Then there are the many scores of terms used by shepherds from one district to another. I recall the old farmer once saying, "Yon ewe's getten a bursenbelly, and her lamb's a cuckoo. Sithy, an' she's a grimetface!" The term 'bursenbelly' is used in some parts to describe a 'dropped' or sagging belly, a 'cuckoo' is a lamb born later than the middle of April, and a 'grimetface' is another term for a greyface (usually the Scottish Greyface, the result of crossing a Border Leicester ram with a Blackface ewe).

Modern dips have reduced the incidence of maggot infestation, but even so the sheep are inspected regularly. Such a round can take several days, but two or three men helped by their dogs lessen the task. Obviously the Pennine shepherd is as dependant on sheepdogs as is the hop-farmer on his stilts. Three active dogs are kept here, together with a young dog, which learns skill from his older brethren and is to some extent assisted by one of his masters —only one of the brothers helps the older dogs to train the young one for to do otherwise would confuse the canine student. Eventually, of course, a good sheepdog can work for more than one master but only really well for one man, the master who instructed him and for whom he invariably has great respect.

As the heather begins to cast its mauve mantle over the heights

during August and the sun begins to set a little less far to the
north-west on each succeeding evening the annual pilgrimage of
grouse shooters takes place. Soon after the twelfth of the month
the men on the farm join with other locals to act as beaters, driving the grouse here and there over the plateau surface, into line for
the gunmen hiding in the butts of hewn peat and heather. Some
place this contrived convenience of beaters and butts under
the heading of 'sport', but I have never understood how an intelligent person can classify it so. Most of the beaters consider it simply
as a source of income and 'a day out'. They do not question the
ethics of such unnecessary slaughter; it certainly makes a change
from dipping sheep or making hay but bears a marked
resemblance, of course, to rounding-up the sheep. Flags fly to
keep ramblers off the area to be shot, and whistles blow; a dog
barks, and a succession of reports mark the flight of grouse put to
the wing by the advancing line of beaters.

Another activity which these farmers sometimes engage in is
less pleasant to them; when vandals leave a broken bottle and a
sheep is lamed they must carry it down to the buildings;
occasionally a fire starts on the heather slopes below the crest of
the plateau and they join in, often after a hard day's work, to beat
it out and so prevent its spread over a large part of the moors.
Another problem of recent years has been the trespass of rock
climbers on to land high above a tributary clough well away from
any right of way. Walls have been pulled down, and loose rocks
from the gritstone crag which has attracted them have plunged
clough-wards and injured several sheep. Sometimes the men have
had to leave important work and climb with dogs up the clough
to send the climbers away. On several occasions the latter have
been abusive and threatened physical violence. Such irresponsible
individuals mercifully make up a relatively small proportion of
those who enjoy the Pennines and other uplands, but here, as else-
where, drastic action has had to be taken to keep this minority
away, and the crag in question has been virtually destroyed by
explosives to keep trespassers away.

Though some visitors to their land—though the farm stands
within the boundaries of a National Park the land is private with

the exception of designated rights of way and areas of 'Open Country'—cause untold inconvenience, these farmers are always ready to help when someone becomes lost or injured. From time to time the men have gone out in the worst weather conditions to help in the search for a lost party last seen on the plateau.

On a winter evening many years ago a knock came at the farmhouse door which set the sheepdogs barking. It was a policeman who had come up from the town in the valley, cycling on the frozen track from the main road where he could, and carrying the bicycle over drifts; it had snowed hard the previous day, and a hard frost through the following night had made a good base for the snow showers which had fallen during this day. Now the wind had dropped, and a half-moon came and went behind occasional high clouds. The policeman brought the news that two men had set off that morning from the next valley to the north, telling the landlord of the inn where they had parked their car that they would be back by three or four o'clock. It was eight o'clock when the landlord informed the police, and immediately this officer had set off to start a search from this side of the plateau, hoping that the men at the farm would join him. Other searchers would follow the route that the lost ramblers had proposed to take when talking to the publican, and a third party had been alerted and they would cross the plateau from the south-east.

The two brothers put on boots and overcoats while their mother and wives prepared flasks and food. Soon the little party set off up the deeply-shadowed clough, the policeman and the two farmers. The going was good, for what snow had fallen that day had blown into small drifts, leaving the frozen crust of earlier snow exposed. For a mile and a half the clough winds up eastwards at a steady angle, and then there is a short, steep slope where the line of the Roman track gains the crest of the plateau. On this steep section the moon was hidden by the slope, and the going was very difficult because ice had formed in wide streaks. On several occasions they fell and slipped on this hidden ice, but after a quarter of an hour the difficulty was crossed, and the little party stood on the edge of the white world, a lunar plateau of unbelievable beauty and silence. Over to the north rises a 2,039-foot-high prominence, which looked like a high mountain in this light.

"It's possible that they are over in the big hollow," said the policeman, his breath steaming out in the frosty air. He was indicating the great depression which occupies the centre of the plateau. The farmers agreed for they knew the topography of this area intimately. The policeman flashed his lamp in a wide arc and they listened; but nothing broke the complete silence of the night. Soon they were feeling cold and began to move over towards the summit of the 2,039-foot eminence which was about a mile away to the north. Breasting the top of a deep channel, where surface water normally drains between peat banks but which was now frozen hard and white, one of the farmers fancied he heard voices. The party stood still and listened.

"There! Voices somewhere near the summit," said the policeman. "It may be the search party from the northern side." All agreed that if it was they had made very good time because that party would have had a longer walk from that northern side. Eventually lights were seen on the top, and soon both parties joined up. It was now one o'clock and the moon was disappearing behind ominous-looking clouds which raced up from the north-west.

"It's gone milder," someone said. "Yes", said a policeman, "and the wind's getting up." Cloud, wind, and a rise in temperature are sure indications in these conditions of imminent snowfall, and, sure enough, only five minutes after the first heavy clouds had obscured the moon, the first flecks of snow were blown on to the summit. Everyone agreed that the only course left open to them was to go down while the going was satisfactory. They did so, but not without the difficulties of descending steep, frozen slopes with snow blowing into their faces. When the combined party reached the farm it was almost three o'clock and an inch of new snow had fallen. Their relief can be imagined when they were told that an hour before the police had telephoned to say that the lost pair had stumbled out of the snowy night a mile from their parked car. They had become lost during the late afternoon when a snow shower had overtaken them on the plateau. Eventually they had

Winter evening, Saddleworth

struggled down in the moonlight but had taken two hours to find their whereabouts, being without torch or compass.

With the formation of a proper mountain rescue organization these farmers rarely find themselves called upon to help in a search for lost walkers. Their attitude has always been one of annoyance that strangers should cause them such inconvenience, but they helped because of a basic humanity and because they knew that occasionally a search is not caused by sheer ignorance or thoughtlessness.

Winter evenings are not usually so exciting, and the greatest activity which normally occurs is the suckling of an early lamb or the last look at a sick ewe or calf in the cow-byre before bed. It is not so long ago that the long winter evenings were passed in home-made pleasures; in embroidery for the women, water-colour painting and jig-saws for the children and the carving of sheeps' horns to ornament the heads of shepherds' crooks. With the coming of a battery wireless much of this entertainment continued, but after the electricity came by overhead cables from the main road things changed. A television was purchased, and most evenings were revolutionized. The first people to agree that this change has not been a 100 per cent improvement are the family. Like so many northern hill farmers who have been working hard in the fresh air all day they know it is so easy to sit back and half watch, half doze.

"My grandfather and even my father would have called an evening's viewing of television a wicked waste of time, and I'm inclined to agree—except on a few occasions," said one brother. He believes that television is more responsible for speeding-up the approach of old age than any other single factor of the modern world, because so many people are content to sit and watch "rubbish of no value" all evening and every evening. But the coming of electricity has been a great boon to both the hill farmer and his wife, and I know of no one who would willingly return to the complications of lighting of house and buildings by paraffin lamps.

"I think we were more inventive before we got power to the
10

Derwent Edge and Ladybower Reservoir from Win Hill

farm; we are more likely to sit back and do nothing now," is one brother's appraisal of the situation. However, winter evenings still bring their crises in the form of difficult calvings, a power line down or frozen water pipes. One thing which has not changed is the whistle of the wind on a corner of the house when it is blowing from the south-west, and the tattoo which rain makes on the living-room windows when driven from the north-west.

Below the farm is a semi-circular reservoir covering several acres, built a century ago to provide water-power for one of the mills at the lower end of the clough, near the town. Around part of this lake rhododendrons were planted, and these have matured to provide a lovely backcloth, their lower branches overhanging the surface. In early summer the pink blooms are massed and reflected in the water, giving the area below the farm the appearance of an ornamental park laid out by a great landscape gardener of the eighteenth century.

Early summer is a time of great charm hereabouts. The rough pastures across the clough are dotted with hawthorn bushes, and at this season are plastered white with bloom. The air is fragrant with their heady scent, and from some hidden corner above a trickling beck the call of the newly-arrived cuckoo sounds across the valley. It is on such a day that the women and children climb the clough with baskets and spread a cloth on the bilberry moor. Tea is taken on the heights beneath a dazzling sky, and life on a Pennine hill farm would not be exchanged by the participants for anything on earth.

CHAPTER XVII

PENNINE VILLAGES

ANYONE familiar with Pennine country will know that settlements are widely spread over the land; the hills and valleys are dotted with farms, hamlets and larger villages. There are, of course, districts where most people live in concentration but the familiar Pennine pattern is one of wide dispersal of settlements. The explanation for this pattern is not so simple as would at first seem to be the case. Several factors have played a part, some together and some separate, in different areas of the region.

Some villages, like several in Wharfedale, have grown up around farms developed originally by monastic bodies in the Middle Ages. These farms and outlying barns contained a nucleus of workers—monks and others—and through the passage of time other dwellings were gathered around them and families multiplied.

Even in this well-watered upland the presence of a "spring line" (a natural string of springs where ground water rose to the surface) has sometimes dictated the location of one or several villages. A good example of such development is the long line of farms and cottages overlooking the upper waters of the Eden at Mallerstang Common. Likewise many of the villages of the White Peak are located near the bottom of a limestone valley or by a reliable spring.

As the troubled times following the invasions of the Romans and the Saxons were forgotten men were free to spread themselves widely over the land which they were to farm. In this way we can understand the outward spread from concentrated settlements to outlying homesteads which typifies much of the Pennine hill country.

Then there is the well known fact of human geography, the relation of difficult, rugged terrain to the isolated holding. The poor soils tend to reduce the human population, each farm and small-holding making use of a small pocket of better soil. In the valleys where there is generally better soil the settlements take the form of village clusters—one need not go farther afield than Wensleydale to see such a pattern. Here there are many nuclear villages close to the fertile soils associated with the River Ure and its dale; Hawes, Bainbridge, Askrigg, Aysgarth, West Witton and the rest are in sharp contrast to the isolated farms scattered at infrequent intervals on the higher ground to the north and south of the dale.

With such facts in mind the settlement pattern of the Pennines can be more readily understood. But remember that no two villages grew up for exactly the same reasons, each is, to some extent, unique.

Two general physical village types emerge. The first is that usually called a 'linear village'. It is a settlement which has grown up along an important route-way, the houses and other buildings stretching a considerable length in relation to the depth or width of the village. Good examples of this type are not frequent in the Pennines. One of the best is the Wensleydale market centre of Hawes. The village grew up here alongside the main road crossing the Pennines between Sedbergh and Leyburn at a suitable water-ing place where Duerley Beck winds down to the north just above the flood plain of the River Ure. Linear development was natural for the road (then merely a trackway) traverses along the river terraces, most convenient features for building along.

The second village type is 'nucleated', often referred to as squared or rounded villages. This type is more common than the former type in Pennine country, the buildings generally surround-ing a green—as at Bainbridge in Wensleydale; or a church com-pound—as at Stainforth in Ribblesdale; or a pond—as at Harting-ton in the Peak District; or, maybe, around a market place in some of those villages which have grown into towns—as at Settle. Occasionally it is possible to trace the shape of a protective

stockade in the resulting village shape. Some of the northernmost settlements of our region conform to the square stockade
which once surrounded them and protected them from attacks
from the invading Scots. From such a primitively protected river-
side settlement the present Teesdale town of Barnard Castle
developed.

But whatever their shape and their origin the villages of the
Pennines have characteristics and atmosphere which makes them
peculiar; they could not, for instance, be mistaken for villages of
the Cotswolds, mid-Wales or even the Lake District. Not only is
the architecture individualistic, their inhabitants are people of
these particular hills. Go to lovely villages like Muker and Keld in
Swaledale or to Dent Town in breathtaking Dentdale to the
west; the inhabitants live very much as did their parents and
grandparents, theirs is a traditional way of life with the earth, the
sky and water as important, forceful elements. As a result each
man and woman is an individual, with a colourful nickname as
often as not—much as Welsh village people have meaningful
nicknames to help identify them when a place has naturally
several people with the same name. However, even in these surprisingly unspoilt places changes there have been. The ubiquitous
motor car has arrived and made communication so much better
with the world beyond the valley-head. The internal combus-
tion engine has also helped to ease the burden of the sheep farmer
and the postman. Yes, the advantages of many modern inventions
have brought help to the lonely places of the northern hills, but
inevitably some of the things that have taken place have not been
good.

Go to the Craven village of Malham at a holiday period. You
will readily see what I mean. Visitors by the hundred pour into
the place, most of them in cars or coaches and the once-peaceful
and pretty limestone village below Malham Cove and Gordale
Scar is over-run and its atmosphere spoilt. Malham on a Bank
Holiday week-end in summer is a dreadful place. Such popularity
has, naturally, brought greater prosperity to the areas involved
and the tourist industry is one of the main occupations in some of
the better known districts like Craven. Even so, villages like

Malham and Grassington are changed and often vulgarized places when compared to the quieter ways shown on photographs taken only twenty years ago.

Many Pennine villages near enough to the industrial centres have become little more than dormitories for town people who have sufficient wealth to live in the country, but few of them are country folk at heart and the villages of their adoption suffer as a result.

This fact is particularly true in the lower Wharfe valley, the upland areas bordering south-eastern Lancashire and in the Peak District. It is in such districts that several villages known to me have lost all their former character, most of the old families have gone and the present inhabitants live in splendid isolation, driving in and out of the village and seeing little of village life and the beautiful land about them. This is real tragedy, even though a particular village may well enjoy much more material wealth than formerly.

Until recent times life centred upon the village shop, the church and chapel and, sometimes, upon the railway station. The former stationmaster at Horton-in-Ribblesdale, Jim Taylor, has recently written of his life in that Craven village beneath Penyghent, where much of the village activities took place at the railway station on the Settle-Carlisle route of the former Midland Railway. He was not simply a stationmaster but helped with sheep movements, clearing snow from the lines in winter and inspecting damage in Blea Moor Tunnel down the track towards Carlisle. Pride in a job done well typified the average village workman and Horton-in-Ribblesdale station took first prize in the Best Kept Gardens Competition for seventeen consecutive years, and each year from its start in 1953 the Cleanliness and Tidiness Competition. Such skill and devotion is typical of the true life of a dalesman.

Life in small, upland communities means that everyone is known to his neighbours. This may not always be a good thing and gossip can be a wicked thing, but most country folk know that the full knowledge they have about all and sundry is usually a comfort and an anchor in life. True village people of the

Pennines know that they belong among their own and could not live happily away from their own nook beneath the old, familiar hill shapes.

The news at the time of writing that British Railways intend to close twelve stations on the line between Settle and Carlisle in 1969 was indeed sad for both the local people and the numberless ramblers and other visitors to the lovely country on both sides of the railway. Among these stations—rendered as unmanned halts quite recently—are those at Horton, Ribblehead, Garsdale and Dent. If this rail link is broken then Ribblehead, for instance, will have its public transport reduced to a bus on Tuesdays and Saturdays only. Though it may be true that no great numbers of dales folk use the stopping trains regularly it is the fact that, to quote a village shopkeeper, "people do not feel so cut off when they know there are two trains a day to Skipton from just up the road." By the time this chapter appears in print the British Railways Board will have bowed to the outcry against these closures or they will have ignored it and added another nail to the coffin of the normal dales way of life.

Life still goes on in its traditional way in the remotest villages and hamlets, but how much longer? The motor car and the Land-Rover, electricity and the tractor have helped to make lonely farmers' lives easier but the basic way goes on as before. Take Halton Gill, for instance, a fine stone hamlet near the head of Littondale, a tributary of Wharfedale. It is a tiny collection of farms, complete with its own old church. Then there is the Peakland hamlet of Alport, in the lonely Alport Dale off the Woodlands Valley. But that is fast emptying and a new Wardens' Briefing Centre and Youth Hostel envisaged for the place will alter its character completely. The problem facing these relatively inaccessible villages is de-population and an ageing remaining population. So the pattern emerging is one of Pennine villages altered in character largely due to increased wealth and an in-flow of outsiders, and of the remotest villages dying due to that very inaccessibility which has allowed them to retain their hill flavour for so long.

All is not yet lost, of course, and village life in the Pennines is still ten times pleasanter than that in the nearest towns and sterile suburbs of red brick and concrete. The secret is that true village people are still close to the mother earth.

CHAPTER XVIII

PENNINE NOTABLES

THE industrial conurbations of Lancashire and the West Riding have been the homes of innumerable men and women for whom the Pennines have exercised an irresistible attraction. Some of them have given their lives to the hills as a result of that early proximity, and Fred Heardman of Edale is one of the best known. Now in his seventies, he originated in south Manchester, and his experience of serious rambling goes back to pre-Great War days. His passion for walking has never abated, and it is to him we owe many of the classic routes of the Pennines. Take, for example, the 'Double Marsden to Edale' and the now well-known 'Three Inns' —from the Isle of Skye above Holmfirth, via the Snake Inn to the Cat and Fiddle above the Goyt Valley—which Fred Heardman invented and covered many times. The list of ingenious high-level rambles owed to this robust character is far too long to detail here, but I must mention the 'Edale to Hebden Bridge' (first done in 1922, measuring 38 miles and taking only nine hours in walking time), 'Penistone to Ashbourne' and the 70-mile 'Colne to Rowsley' (done with two companions in 1926). Before moving to Edale, where he was for many years the landlord of the Nag's Head Inn, Fred Heardman lived at the guest-house called Tunstead, under Kinder Scout's western slopes. While at Edale—he now lives in retirement (if that is a fitting description for a septuagenarian who still walks long distances over our Pennine heights and further afield) near the village—he was one of the foremost fighters in the pre-war field of battle waged against those greedy enough to plan a steel works in the lovely Vale of Edale. More recently he has been very active in the development of the Peak

Park Planning Board's Information Centre. This began in a room of his Nag's Head Inn before occupying the new premises at Fieldhead, Edale. For his services to Mountain Rescue he has become a holder of the M.B.E., and everyone who knows this jolly fountain-head of upland knowledge was pleased to hear the news. On most days of the year he can be seen striding off in brown plus-fours up a lonely clough or over the swelling peat moors, where the curlew calls against a tor-dotted horizon. He admits that Bleaklow is his favourite Peak District area nowadays, in the face of the high-density invasion of Kinder Scout by the masses who come by car and train to Edale, particularly at holiday periods.

At the time when Fred Heardman was accomplishing some of his finest walks there was born in one of the less salubrious parts of Manchester a boy who was destined to become the finest rock climber of all time. He it was more than any other individual who was responsible for increasing the standard of difficulty on British and Alpine rock routes to a point previously thought impossible without resort to artificial aids. Early days on the gritstone moors of the Peak District led to the first attempts on the gritstone edges with his mother's discarded clothes-line, foreshadowing the great days on gritstone when new routes like Valkyrie on Froggatt Edge and the Right Unconquerable Crack on Stanage Edge were invented by Brown and his friends. Long days and nights on the moors and edges, and longer routes on Welsh cliffs with very hard routes like Cenotaph Corner on Dinas Cromlech led to the Alps and the Karakoram and Himalayas. In 1955 our Mancunian reached the summit of Kangchenjunga (28,150 feet), third highest in the world. He is, of course, none less than Joe Brown; and he is the first to admit the importance of the Pennines to his career as one of the world's leading mountaineers. The proximity of those brown ridges, plateaux and edges in early youth led to an interest no less keen than that evident in Fred Heardman and other pioneers and (later) notables.

On no group of natives more than those with a bent for creative writing, painting and sculpture have the Pennines exerted a stronger motivation to expression. The powerful skies and definite shapes of the hills have inspired many noble imaginations, to an extent we can never calculate. Their flavour of wildness-next-to-home sums up their character, great uplands adjacent to nestling farms and villages and bigger towns where the sensitive man can never be long forgetful of their presence and influence.

The once-Derbyshire, now-Yorkshire, village of Norton lies immediately south of Sheffield, and from it, through the trees near the parish church, the swelling outlines of Eastmoor can be seen a few miles to the west. Here was born, in April 1781, Francis Chantrey. From the tiny cottage where his family lived, Francis daily drove a donkey down Derbyshire Lane to Sheffield with the milk, little dreaming that he was to become a portrait painter of distinction and later the outstanding sculptor of his age. Many of his fine pencil sketches of Peak District scenery still exist, acquired a few years ago by Sheffield Art Galleries. They were drawn in 1815 as roughs for Ebenezer Rhodes' notable work called *Peak Scenery* which was published in several volumes between 1818 and 1823. Here are wonderfully simple sketches of Froggatt Bridge, Haddon Hall, Eyam Village and Dovedale. It seems that Chantrey did not elaborate on them, rather leaving it to the skilled engravers, W. B. and George Cooke, to add the necessary detail, light and shade and marginal extensions when etching the final work for Rhodes' book. Later Chantrey abandoned portrait painting for sculpture, the medium for which he is best remembered, and in 1818 he was elected R.A. and knighted in 1835. It is well known that he believed in streamlining the production of even his important sculpture with the help of several assistants, so leaving a minimum of craftwork to himself. Some of his finest work rests in or near his well-loved southern Pennines; for instance, the monument in Ilam church near the River Dove and four miles from Ashbourne, which represents the aged David Pike Watts on his death-bed and attended by his daughter and her family. One of his finest creations is the monument under the east window of the south choir aisle in Lichfield Cathedral depicting the "Sleeping Children"—the daughters of the Rev. William Robinson. Chantrey died in 1841 in circumstances very much altered from those donkey-days down Derbyshire Lane, with the blue backgroud of Totley Moss and Lodge Moor across the Sheaf Valley.

A modern counterpart of Chantrey in this context is L. S. Lowry. The grand old man of modern British painting lives in splendid isolation in mediocre urban surroundings on the west side of the Pennines, in that muddle of mill towns between Glossop and Manchester. Of course, his stick-figure-populated canvasses are not Pennine in the true sense of the word, but often a far horizon beyond the mill chimneys and ranks of roofs shows that world to be not far distant. The subject of most of his work relies, basically, upon those hills—without them the mills and the people would never have cramped those west-facing Lancastrian slopes and valley-floors. It is amazing to consider that compositions like "Scene in a Manufacturing Town" (painted in 1922) earned the artist a relatively small income, yet when sold recently at auction that oil fetched 4,400 guineas and not a penny will go to the genius which created it. To men like L. S. Lowry who live to see their work become valuable there is a disturbing facet to the world which later appreciates them, rarely benefiting them financially to the extent deserved.

In an earlier age there came to Pennine country a handful of great landscape artists, and they have left a fine record of the scenery which they saw. John Sell Cotman came to Teesdale in the summer of 1805 and absorbed the great fullness of natural beauty in the vicinity of Rokeby Park, overlooking the confluence of the River Greta with the River Tees three miles below Barnard Castle. He was only 23 years old, and these waters from the hills (and the valleys in which they ran) made a great impression upon the artist who was destined to become Professor of Drawing at King's College, London. Among them were the watercolours entitled "Distant View of Greta Bridge" and "The Meeting of the Tees and Greta".

The other great artist who visited the northern hill country during late Georgian times was J. M. W. Turner. When 42 or 43 years old—in 1817 or 1818—he started the drawings to illustrate what was to become the finest topographical book ever published. Turner had previously illustrated books of history on the Whalley and Craven districts by Dr. Whitaker, and the new work, to be entitled *History of Richmondshire*, was to be the outstanding work of this local historian. The artist received twenty-five guineas for each of the water-colour drawings from the publishers, and each is in the typically charming style of his 'Yorkshire period', which extended from 1809 to about 1820. The period marked his transition from the use of dark colours to lighter, more natural ranges of colour. The owner of Farnley Hall in Wharfedale was a patron and friend of Turner's, and the latter often stayed there, drawing the charming scenery and effects of light in this dale. Ruskin later wrote in his *Modern Painters* the following:

> It is, I believe, to these broad, wooded steeps and swells of the Yorkshire downs that we, in part, owe the singular massiveness that prevails in Turner's mountain drawing, and gives it one of its chief elements of grandeur . . . I am in the habit of looking to the Yorkshire drawings and indicating one of the culminating points of Turner's career.

Probably the finest water-colour in the *History of Richmondshire*, and one of the most consummate works of the artist is "The Crook of the Lune". Though the subject was obviously a very difficult one, Turner dealt with the extensive landscape bounding this beautiful Lancashire river, where it makes its famous sudden turn, in great detail. The yellow-browns, pale, sunny greens and the swirling waters, the minuteness of detail and the excellence of the viewpoint are perfectly united to harmonize the composition as a whole. By 1827, when "Barnard Castle" was drawn, Turner's treatment of a subject had been simplified so that a yellow light pervades the river and invades the foreground vegetation, the ruins beyond little more than a pale grey wash. However, the scene is set as no one else has ever managed to set it; the imagination does the rest.

But who is the best-known Pennine child? Which son or daughter of the northern hills? Surely not a single individual genius but a family trio, those literary giants of their own wild, upland, lonely world—the sisters Brontë. Much has been written of the life and works of Charlotte (1816–55), Emily (1818–48) and Anne (1820-49). Suffice to say that these girls would undoubtedly have written, no matter where they had been born and lived. The fact that they lived in the West Riding Pennines meant that their works were strongly Pennine in character—mill town and moorland farm, upland intake land and gritstone tors, these are the properties for their remarkable novels. All three girls were born at Thornton, a part of Bradford today, where their father was a curate. Anne was only four months old when the family moved to Haworth in 1820, and Charlotte, the eldest, was only four years old; so it was Haworth and the country about that impressed itself upon their sensitive imaginations. One hundred and twenty years after her untimely death, it is Emily Brontë who is considered the greatest genius because of the originality and timelessness of her *Wuthering Heights*. In another chapter I have referred to the probable geographical location of this lonely farm on the heights above Haworth. That this extremely shy and outwardly composed young woman could turn out such a story of full-blooded emotions is truly remarkable and tells us much of her concealed, inner self. The story of the three Brontë sisters is one quite as remarkable as any which they created. Lonely and stricken with misfortune, they died while still young—Anne was 29, Emily 30 and Charlotte 39—victims of the weak constitutions which had dogged them throughout life. Today Haworth is almost entirely given over as a Brontë museum and rather disappointing for such treatment. The parsonage above the church is the official museum, and rightly so, but the 100,000 visitors which annually come to Haworth can see much which the Brontë family would not have known; the gift shops, tea shops and other relatively new and unnecessary accompaniments detract from the true character of this hill-set town above the Worth Valley. Brontë this and Brontë that, at every end and turn, but it is a state of affairs for which no one in particular is responsible but rather a trend caused by the great increase in popularity of this literary shrine. If the pilgrims did not demand and support such commercialism Haworth would be more the place its famous inhabitants knew long ago, and less self-conscious.

Not far away in these West Riding uplands lives Dr. Phyllis

Bentley, who is best known for her research into the Brontës and for her many books and plays on Pennine life and people.

Besides the giants known to everyone there are many less famous notables, men who either never reached a pinnacle like the Brontë sisters or whose life's work was not destined to be popular to the general public. Men who, nevertheless, were great and must not slide into oblivion. All were influenced by the hills of their birth.

There was Charles Waterton, who in later life returned to his ancestral home at Walton Hall, near Wakefield, and continued his great life work of looking at wild things. Born in 1782, he lived for a long time in South America, and in the years before his death in 1865 allowed his Yorkshire home to become a sanctuary for wild animals and birds.

Adam Sedgwick was born three years after Charles Waterton in the lovely village of Dent. He has already been mentioned in this book so it is sufficient to recall here that this lad of the northern dales rose to be the foremost geologist of his day, occupying the chair of geology (as Woodwardian Professor) at Cambridge for many years. His particular claim to fame centred upon his study of and interest in the oldest rocks, especially those bearing fossiliferous remains. He died at the age of 87, having lived long enough to see considerable advances in geological knowledge, much of it based upon his own earlier research.

At Sheffield in 1826, close to the southern Pennines, was born Henry Clifton Sorby, whose chief claim to fame is as the developer of microscopic analysis of rocks, and towards the end of his life—he died in 1908—he was known as 'the Father of Microscopic Petrography'. The Sorby Natural History Society of Sheffield perpetuates the memory of this great Pennine naturalist and scientist. Another Sheffield man, born over forty years earlier who has a learned society named in his memory, was Joseph Hunter (1783–1861), and the society is the Hunter Archaeological Society. He was a Presbyterian Minister but is best known for his several books on the topography and history of the southernmost Pennines and Hallamshire, Sheffield.

Henry Briggs was born 270 years before Sorby at Warely, near

Halifax. It was, and still is, an unremarkable little place, but Briggs was a most remarkable young man. He was a mathematical genius and went to Cambridge, rose to become Savilian Professor at Oxford and wrote the *Arithmetica Logarithmica*, which introduced to the world the use of logarithms. For that he has been called "the greatest benefactor the Navy ever had". His interest in seafaring was considerable, and he became a patron to Luke Foxe's Arctic explorations; for that, and his contributions to navigation, Foxe named an island group in Briggs' honour a year after his death in 1630.

Though William Congreve (1669–1729) was born at Bardsey seven miles north-east of Leeds, it is, I hope, permissible to stretch our region so as to mention him. Anyway, in that low county between the Aire and the Wharfe the high land rising to the gritstone moors is quite clear away to the west. Congreve is one of a handful of the greatest comedy writers of any age, and his illuminating plays are comparable with the work of the caricaturist Thomas Rowlandson of a later period, for they expose satirically the fashions and moods of the 'better classes' of the day. At 24 his plays *The Old Bachelor* (written in a grotto by the River Dove) and *The Double Dealer* obtained immediate success. Two years later his mastery of brilliant repartee was shown in his best-known play *Love for Love*, later to be called the finest prose comedy in the English language. His last play was completed when he was only 31, though he lived for another twenty-nine years.

Before the Industrial Revolution there was less disparity between the population of an upland region like the Pennines and the lowlands because of the Pennine region's greater population relative to the rest of England in those days; compared with more recent times it appeared to produce a disproportionate number of eminent men. Many of these notables moved away from their native Pennines on attaining importance, but their roots were in the hills of their birth. Conversely, we see today numerous notables taking to the Pennines in an effort to flee the monotony and mediocrity of urbanization.

In that age of religious re-awakening which occurred in the late seventeenth and eighteenth centuries it is not surprising that these

Hathersage Church from the Hall

uplands produced a noteworthy group of fervent theologians and divines.

There was the boy born at Old Haugh End, Halifax in 1630, who became a most popular preacher. His name was John Tillotson. Educated at Clare College, Cambridge, he was a fervent Calvinist, but at the Restoration of Charles II in 1660 he submitted to the Act of Uniformity and in 1662 married a niece of Oliver Cromwell. This was a turning point in his life, for now he rose rapidly in office. After holding the positions of Rector of Kedington, Suffolk, Dean of Canterbury and Dean of St. Paul's in London, John Tillotson succeeded Archbishop Sancroft at Canterbury in 1691. This northern divine was well known for his tolerance, but he is best remembered for his outstanding sermons from the pulpit. It has been authoritatively stated that Tillotson's sermons "were regarded as the standard of finished oratory" before his death in November 1694.

At Oulton, near Leeds, in 1662, and within sight of the West Riding Pennines, was born Richard Bentley. A man with a brilliant mind, he had the disposition of a fighter for what he believed was right, and his life was punctuated by verbal battles with other scholars. The most remarkable was the controversy with Charles Boyle of Oxford which centred on the question of ancient and modern learning and is known as the 'Phalaris Controversy'. Sir William Temple, the famous diplomatist, and his secretary, Jonathan Swift, became involved and stoutly took Boyle's side. The story of the dispute gave Swift the subject for his well-known work published in 1704 and entitled *The Battle of the Books*. At the age of 38 Bentley became master of Trinity College, Cambridge, and seventeen years later he combined this post with that of Regius Professor of Divinity. He died in July 1742 at the age of 80 as one of Yorkshire's most highly esteemed sons.

Six years after the birth of Richard Bentley there was born at Wakefield a boy called Joseph Bingham who rose to the pinnacle of fame as a theologian, largely through his great scholarship as shown in his *Origines Ecclesiasticae* (the History of Christianity). A year after Bentley's death another theologian was born at Giggleswick, near Settle. He was William Paley, who became a moral

11

philosopher. After graduating from Christ's College, Cambridge, as Senior Wrangler he stayed on to become a fellow and tutor. His best known written work was *Evidences of Christianity*, and until 1920 this was a subject for examination at Cambridge. After ten years in residence at Cambridge, John Paley became sub-dean of Lincoln and rector of Bishop Wearmouth, in which offices he died at the age of 62 in 1805.

But up and down the Pennines to this day are innumerable men and women of the land, born and bred in the valleys and on the hill slopes. In contrast to men like Joe Brown who have been attracted to the hills by the exercise, beauty, thrills or the wild life (or a combination of these things), these upland natives are notable in their own right, true Pennine men; practical and down-to-earth in the best and natural sense. Such a man is Sam Throup, who lives at his birthplace, Far Fold Farm, High Bradley, near Skipton. Here is a real Dalesman, full of character and maybe in spirit a left-over from an age which has virtually passed. Now in his seventies and living alone since the death of his artist-wife, Sam Throup is a fund of knowledge concerning the past and the present Pennine scene. At High Bradley there was once a smithy for the production of cow shoes. These metal plates had holes in one side for nails to pass into the cows' cloven hooves, leaving one side of the hoof to spread during walking. The reason for this smithy being at High Bradley is that cattle from the limestone hills of Craven were sold at the market here and were often faced thereafter with a long walk on to the Plain of York, maybe 40 miles beyond the market. Sam still farms thirty-eight acres and, unlike so many Pennine farmers, spends time looking at the wild things about him. "I've talked to tewits (pewits or lapwings) all mi life. I like to hear 'em in t'spring o' t'year. It maks you think you're paddlin' through t'winter varry nicely."

CHAPTER XIX

SPACE FOR ALL?

THE upland ridge forming the subject of this book is not unlimited in area. Two centuries ago the inhabitants of the West Riding, the Forest of Trawden, Teesdale or the upper Tyne Valley may have thought so. The farmers of the Woodlands Valley in the Peak District would have considered their lower pastures the safest place on earth, a haven from the unknown world beyond. The mist-shrouded moors and edges which over-shadowed them were their own country, traversed by only their own stock and neighbours and the occasional brave traveller. The sheep upon Cross Fell saw their shepherd occasionally and no one else in their whole wide world of distant horizons. The farming communities at Barley, in Lancashire, and at Malham in the West Riding, were close-knit and saw little from beyond their respective parish boundaries to trouble them. The days of warring bands was at an end; the Civil War had ended a century before. What, I wonder, would their thoughts have been had they seen in some accurate fortune-teller's globe the changes destined to overtake their Pennine land in the future?

No one can deny that many parts of this lovely watershed area are not so lovely as formerly. The Industrial Revolution made great inroads into the lovely countryside of the central and southern Pennines, from east and west. The valleys belched—and still belch—smoke, fumes and pollution in general over the surrounding moors and intervening farmland. We have come to take the old-established rape of the hills by our Georgian and, more especially, Victorian forebears—the mill dams, the tall chimneys, the railways and their ventilation shafts, and the new turnpike roads—rather for granted. The parts long desecrated are no longer mourned; the Worth Valley, Littleborough and Ripponden we know as industrial, and we keep away from their grimy surroundings whenever possible. But there is a new evil, another danger not considered two or three generations ago, which is more insidious and threatens even more seriously than did the mill chimneys of long ago. It is the combined onslaught of individuals with new-found leisure and authorities with apparently limitless power to take over our heritage of high land for the development of new roads, reservoirs and the like. The former contingent have as their greatest weapon the motor car, ubiquitous machine of our age, which carries those who barely deserve such freedom to the very heart of the hills. The coming of the car to the masses who drive in long ranks and see little of real interest to them, armed with tables and chairs, newspapers and transistor radios, has spoilt quite large parts of the Pennines where public roads enter steep hill-country. Few of this mass show an intelligent interest in the land about them, they are there for a change, for something to do on Sunday afternoons (many awaiting the inevitable escape to the open door of the public house) and see little of the world of the wild about them. In fact, I know full well that the vast majority of such trippers are in the country for an hour or two but not of the country; it is an alien land. The motor car can be used to advantage, of course, in the Pennines if it is used intelligently; it can be a useful servant to take one to a remote or distant point from where an area may be explored on foot. Few of the motorists seen on Pennine roads at weekends, though, seem to know anything of the unspeakable pleasure that any of this upland area can offer to the initiated.

But before looking at the modern trends in the utilization of the region for leisure there is another matter worthy of consideration. As more people visit these uplands for pleasure, so fewer people live in certain areas due to the influences of economic and social change. This is particularly true in the northern Pennines, in the vast upland region between the Tweed and the Wharfe. The Agriculture Act, 1967, authorized the establishment of rural development boards. The one with which we are here concerned

is that known as the Northern Pennines Rural Development
Board, which will have surveillance over an area of 1,984,000
acres in Northumberland, Cumberland, Durham, Lancashire,
Westmorland and the North and West Ridings of Yorkshire, an
area exceeding that of the entire West Riding by 198,000 acres.
The object of such development boards is to "work a thriving,
prosperous rural area"; in other words, to prevent further depopulation in remote districts and, if possible, to help increase the
population towards pre-Great War numbers. In the northern
Pennines the chief aim will be to develop farming and forestry,
making agricultural holdings more economic and remunerative.
The Northern Pennines Rural Development Board—hereafter the
N.P.R.D.B.—is also charged with "the conservation of scenic
amenities and the provision of better facilities for visitors".

At the time of writing there is considerable opposition to the
setting-up of the N.P.R.D.B. on several counts. Firstly, there is
the argument that if more and more facilities are provided for
visitors the majority of this influx will interfere with the improve-
ments to farming and forestry and will benefit only hotel owners
and shop-keepers. There is a valid argument here, for it seems
obvious that only those who want to come without all the para-
phernalia of artificial attractions should be encouraged, and they
need little or no encouragement anyway. The keen rambler, the
rock climber and speleologist, the geographer and biologist will
come no matter what the weather and irrespective of how many
picnic sites or broad roads there are awaiting him. Secondly, as
noted in a leading article in the *Yorkshire Post* in March 1968, "the
hill farmers with long traditions of sturdy independence and
winning a living against the odds can hardly be expected to look
with enthusiasm at the establishment of a body able to interfere
with plans for the disposal of land". This resentment is prompted
by the fact that the N.P.R.D.B. will have powers to control trans-
fers of land so that encouragement is given to the formation of
what it considers more viable farms and "to prevent the formation
of what it deems new uneconomic farms". Although the Agriculture Act, 1967, provides balances and checks on what the new
board may do, there is much disapproval, particularly among

those with agricultural interests in this extensive area. They do not like the sound of the clause which states that the board may find it difficult "to agree to a proposal to break up a holding" and which goes on to explain that the board may look upon the sale of a small farming unit which (to them) did not appear to possess an economic future with disfavour and so attempt to use the land "to increase the area of some other farm or farms and thus secure a better living for the occupiers concerned".

Skipton Rural Council has opposed the formation of the N.P.R.D.B. Members of this council have rightly argued that such a body would inevitably become "a tyrant" and, anyhow, an uneconomic hill farm dies naturally, and the land is almost always then joined to nearby holdings.

The new board is planned so that it can exert a strong influence over the sparsely-populated hills of the northern Pennines. It is entitled to acquire by agreement any land within the region and is empowered "to manage, improve, farm, sell, let or otherwise deal with" land so acquired—and this may involve "a farming business or farm stock". On the credit side must be mentioned that the board can give financial help (by grant and/or loan) to improve communications and public services. But its power to create new caravan and camping sites will cause frowns on many faces. At the time of writing another fear being expressed is that there may be insufficient farming representation on the board, with a consequent repetition of "the National Park fiasco where there is no farming representation", to quote an official of the West Riding branch of the N.F.U. A former Minister of Agriculture, Fisheries and Food expressed his supreme faith in the good which the new rural development boards could do in areas like the northern Pennines. Such boards must contain a good proportion of farming representation to be run at all effectively, that is a matter of common sense. Whether the N.P.R.D.B. will turn out to be a tyrannical white elephant or an effective power of good in the depopulated uplands will be shown by the passage of time.

Then there are reservoirs. In an upland area singularly lacking in natural lakes the presence of some reservoirs is desirable simply from a scenic point of view, that is, providing those introduced waters do not destroy natural or man-made scenery of equal or greater merit. The regions concerned here are the northern and southern Pennines for the limestone uplands of the centre are unsuitable for the construction of reservoirs. The industry and dense populations of south Lancashire and the West Riding and the close proximity of suitable gritstone valleys have meant the use of many lovely south Pennine valleys on both sides of the main watershed for water storage. The greater distance to the industrial north-east and north-west and the presence of the Lake District not far away has meant that the valleys of the northern Pennines have not been utilized to anywhere near such an extent. However, because of a new shortage of water for industry on Tees-side, a reservoir is being constructed at Cow Green in Upper Teesdale, at the place where Westmorland, the North Riding of Yorkshire and Durham meet. It is in the wild, upland basin above High Force and Cauldron Snout and will supply 9,000 million gallons of water to, in particular, Imperial Chemical Industries far away near the sea. There is tragedy here. Though the reservoir will not curtail the flow of waters over High Force and Cauldron Snout (because it is basically a compensation reservoir, and a steady flow of water will be liberated down the River Tees at most times of the year) the rising waters will drown twenty acres of really remarkable Arctic-Alpine vegetation. Cow Green is not an area of dull moorland—not that any moorland could be dull— but a first-class example of an area of living 'fossil vegetation' which possesses many of the known facts and the secrets of vegetation patterns of long ago. The reservoir is to be completed so that water will be available on Tees-side by the spring of 1971, so the threatened area behind the dam must be studied quickly before all the interesting material is drowned forever. I.C.I. have established what is known as the Teesdale Trust to foster scientific examination before it is too late. Under the chairmanship of Professor A. R. Clapham a committee will co-ordinate the various spheres of study, assisted by the £10,000 grant to be paid by I.C.I. each year for ten years. One of the most urgent pieces of research being undertaken at the time of writing is an investigation into plant succession down the slope which will eventually be flooded.

Another important feature which will be inundated by the water is extensive peat bog, the examination of which can reveal various periods of vegetation change in a district; here, for instance, there are the remains of birch timber and bark at various depths in the peat which show that Upper Teesdale was afforested at least once.

This great upland, which falls eastwards and south-eastwards from the main watershed at Mickle Fell and Dufton Fell, is subject to very low temperatures in winter and is covered to a remarkable extent by soils rich in minerals; just the conditions in which many species of Arctic-Alpine flora flourish. One such species threatened is the Spring Gentian (*Gentiana verna*), with its intense blue flowers, in bloom between April and June on erect stems an inch or more in length. Besides the rare site here in the northern Pennines, this species is only found growing wild in any quantity in the Burren Country of western Ireland. Several species of spiders associated with an Arctic environment inhabit this area, as do dragonflies and moles (the latter being unusual because they live happily at the 2,000 feet contour). Luckily the Teesdale Trust has a mediator in the person of Mr. Tom Buffey. His task is to see that the contractors working for the industrialists in the reservoir construction do not destroy what is important before it has been thoroughly investigated by one or more of the various scientific teams at work in Upper Teesdale. Another facet of Mr. Buffey's work is to see that flora and fauna around the Cow Green site is not interfered with unnecessarily. His job is not an easy one, but, luckily for all lovers of the wild and for the scientist recording his particular data, their ombudsman is dedicated.

In the Peak District the Trent River Authority plans to construct a large new reservoir in the near future in one of six possible sites. Already this proposal has met with opposition from several sides; from landowners, local inhabitants and amenity societies. Peakland has too many lovely valleys already partially or wholly drowned. That some of the six possible sites are in unspoilt gritstone country is to be expected, but two of these are outrageous in the extreme and are to be completely condemned. One is the wide moorland valley of the River Ashop, really Ashop

Clough above its confluence with Lady Clough. Along its length runs the famous Hayfield Path from the Snake Inn to Hayfield by way of Ashop Head, where the Pennine Way crosses from Kinder Scout on to Mill Hill (1,761 feet) and so north-eastwards towards Bleaklow. Several delightful side-cloughs descend into Ashop Clough from the northern slopes, including Within Clough, Red Clough and Upper Gate Clough. High above the valley on the southern side is The Edge, Kinder Scout's northern rampart of millstone grit, and on Black Ashop Moor beneath it are the ruins of the famous shooting cabin. Down by the bank of the river in the main valley—close to the outflow of Upper Gate Clough's stream —are the sad ruins of Ashop Clough shooting cabin which only in recent years has fallen into complete decay. There are few better places in the southern Pennines than here to listen to and see the curlew, the dunlin and other waders during summer months. And another proposed site for the new reservoir is not far away and equally fortunate. It is that valley which cuts deep into central Bleaklow from the south, Alport Dale. If this were eventually chosen as the site for the reservoir I know that there would be an all-out uproar from a great majority of lovers of the area. The secret windings of the upper Dale, the broad bed of the River Alport and the dramatic setting of Alport Castles (Britain's largest landslip) are three of the features of the valley which must not be defaced. There is space here to mention one other proposed site, and that is in very different country on the eastern flank of the Peak District, in the upper Amber Valley above the pretty village of Ashover. The dam would be built on a line of faults so that, besides destroying the beautiful scenery about Brockhurst and Overend, the villagers of Ashover are naturally concerned by the dangers which such a large reservoir might bring to the lower valley and their village.

Quite recently a new reservoir has been completed in the western Peak District, filling the remainder of the Dale of Goyt above the existing Fernilee Reservoir. The whole of this fine grit-stone dale was depopulated when the first reservoir was built by Stockport Corporation before World War II (that is, the whole dale above the impounding dam) so that the collecting grounds would be relatively clean. Many old farms and Errwood Hall itself fell into dereliction at that time, so the building of the Errwood Reservoir in the last year or two has not resulted in any further depopulation. However, it has meant the disappearance of the fine metal suspension bridge carrying the footpath across the head of Fernilee Reservoir and of the ancient pack-horse bridge over the River Goyt. The other old pack-horse bridge a little higher upstream has been dismantled and re-erected a mile and a half higher up, out of the reach of the waters of the new Errwood Reservoir. Another unfortunate loss is the lower section of the drive to Errwood Hall, and many scores of magnificent mature rhododendron bushes and some fine trees have been felled and burnt. A new reinforced concrete bridge carries the re-routed road around the dale now and so to The Street, the old Roman and medieval route over into Cheshire with its wonderful avenue of sweet chestnuts. This new reservoir has cost £1,500,000 and is retained by a 1,000-feet-long earth embankment, which rises to 145 feet above river level. The actual surface area of the reservoir when full is 78 acres, and its capacity is 927 million gallons collected over 3,800 acres of the upper Dale of Goyt.

Here is another example of the way in which steady inroads can be, and are being, made into natural and/or semi-natural upland. With reference to the proposal to select a site for another reservoir, already mentioned above, the Sheffield and Peak District Branch of the Council for the Preservation of Rural England has taken a firm stand and shown that the ignorant claim that such reservoirs are inevitable is not necessarily correct. To quote its official statement:

> No further large-scale flooding of river valleys should be authorized until all other sources of supply have been fully exploited. The time has come to live boldly in the twentieth century, to eliminate waste and use desalination, rather than render our best land and scenery impotent by inundation.

Rambling has undergone an almost complete metamorphosis since the early years of this century. At that time walkers on the heights were few, their legal territory on high ground was severely limited and most of them were educated, professional men and women. The battles with gamekeepers, the scouting and avoidance of shooting parties on the plateaux, the fun derived by the athletic rambler in avoiding angry landowners and their staff in those days is well known. The position has come almost full-circle and the Pennine rambler has a freedom which earlier generations would certainly have envied. Almost full-circle, not completely full-circle because some of the former rights of way, especially over cultivated land at lower elevations on the eastern and western margins of the Pennines have been lost due to lack of use. Many former farm-to-farm paths used essentially by farm staff and families have become neglected and right-of-way over them has been lost. However, we are here largely interested in the higher ground.

At a recent annual meeting of the West Riding area of the Ramblers' Association held at Burley-in-Wharfedale the problem of open space, unspoilt by industrial and other claims, was discussed. The western parts of the Dales National Park contain some of the loveliest wild country in England, a region of sparse population which is unique and must at all costs retain its natural character. The Association meeting urged the need for the creation of a huge central area of this National Park, where 'amenity' should be given priority over agricultural and industrial interests. In other words, the creation of a "vast reservoir of open space". This central area is suggested as being bounded by Mallerstang, Wild Boar Fell and High Cup Nick on the north, by Ingleborough and Whernside on the west, by the fells overlooking Nidderdale on the east and by Barden Fell and Barden Moor on the south. At the same meeting the well-known Yorkshire historian and author, Dr. Arthur Raistrick, president of the West Riding branch, made the case quite clear by stating that "it must be impressed upon Parliament that there are hundreds of thousands of people opposed to any attempt greatly to reduce the number of footpaths and bridleways, and who are expecting the Countryside Bill to give greater protection to public rights of way".

But in our search for freedom and access to the wild places of the Pennines we must not organize things so well that we cannot get away from the sphere of man. I am thinking particularly of the signposting and labelling of all facilities for visitors. In the Peak District there have sprung up a series of green National Park signs at appropriate lay-bys with the ludicrous statement that we are at a "scenic lay-by"! If the motorist has not the sense to know such a fact he has no business to be there at all. The true hill wanderer does not want to be told where he is at every end and turn; it would seem that many of the National Park officers responsible for the welfare of their park are not real countrymen—one certainly gets that impression from time to time.

During the middle and latter half of the last century the com- plexity of railway companies did their fair share to desecrate the Pennines, but the passage of time has healed most of the wounds so that today many consider these routes of particular historic interest, and we often bemoan the closing or lifting of some of the lines. On 1st July 1968 the former Midland Railway's scenic route from Derby to Manchester via Rowsley and Miller's Dale was closed to all traffic for most of its length. At the time of writ- ing plans are afoot for the Peak Park Planning Board to utilize the route through the limestone dales of the River Wye as a broad footpath for visitors. Would there be, I wonder, any great objec- tion to retain one of the two tracks and use it as a private railway to transport the general visitor and the railway enthusiast? There would be scope here for liaison with local education authorities (half of Britain's population live within fifty miles of this National Park) to use the line for the transport of mobile class-rooms, special wagons conveying groups through Peakland on geographi- cal, biological and other excursions. The pre-war railway through the Manifold Valley in eastern Staffordshire now makes a fine, level footpath, the track having been taken away years ago. The recently closed Derby-Manchester line could well be used as a footpath and as a single line track for the purposes just mentioned. It is my per- sonal hope that the Settle-Carlisle route, the finest of all Pennine railways, does not meet the same fate, but if it is finally closed by the British Railways Board it would be wonderful for some far- sighted body to use the line as an enthusiasts' paradise, though the purchase and maintenance of this historic route (even in part) would be prohibitive if recent sale prices of sections of line to private parties are maintained.

All in all, the Pennines are the birthright of everyone and especially so of those living in close proximity to them. Britain's finest long-distance ridge or watershed. Preservation of this region is essential, but needless publicity must surely be a great mistake. Let those who are keenly interested in the heights wander there at will—they are usually responsible individuals—but to advertise and beckon must surely bring those who really have no placed in the Pennines, and then the problems begin. A balance is the answer, a balance of preservation of rural permanence and solitude and defence against attack by greedy commercialism, and a restraint in proclaiming the glories of the hills— if such restraint is lacking in responsible quarters the glory will inevitably fade.

CHAPTER XX

A PENNINE DIARY

THE joys of keeping a diary are normally retrospective. One may look back years later and enjoy again experiences long since forgotten. In all my years of wandering in wild places I have kept records of thoughts and deeds which seemed worth setting down. Below are a random selection of these which are appropriate to the subject of this book.

January

The fall of snow was followed by twenty-four hours of hard frost, and later an icy wind from the north stretched its sharp claws over the land. Fine powder snow blew quickly into sharp-crested drifts, and the windward side of the wood filled up with the white dust.

As I walked after dark through the winter landscape, the half-moon was revealed through a gap in the clouds. Though moonlight does not show colours, it appeared this time that all the world was shot through with various hues of purple-blue. The distant wood's edge looked like pewter, and the snow on the pasture field where I stood was duck-egg.

There, revealed by the quickly passing moonlight, was a bold line of tracks, obviously made by a pheasant and luckily not drifted over by the blowing snow. The tracks ran close to a hedge-bottom and turned towards the middle of the field, where they ended suddenly. The last pair of prints were deeper than the rest as a result of the effort needed to become airborne. Beyond again, the tips of the wing feathers were impressed on the snow as the heavy bird completed its first wing beat. The pheasant must have been startled by something in, or beyond, the hedgerow. It might have been a weasel, a prowling cat or a fox, but all evidence had been drifted over by the blowing snow, and soon the moon was back behind the clouds again.

February

Leaving the light of the farmhouse the other evening, I wheeled my bicycle into the narrow confines of the lane. At first it seemed that my eyes weren't yet accustomed to the darkness, even so it seemed abnormally dark. Rarely do I switch the light on for my journey home over the hills. However, there was absolutely nothing to be seen, and, after wobbling dangerously close to the edge of the lane-side pond, I used the headlamp, faint flicker though it was. Further up the hill I pushed my mount and, without the lamp again, analysed the darkness. There was no sign of anything, and barely any sound. It was a combination of no moon and a thick layer of low cloud which hid the stars—

> No stars, no moon,
> No light of cars
> Upon the distant, hillside road.

Such depths of darkness (or lack of light) were often described in this area as "black as a bag" or "bottom of the well at midnight". Even so all visibility hadn't gone, for, by careful concentration, it was just possible to make out the vague shape of a small oak over the wall above the road, where its arms stood against an area of less dense cloud-cover.

The darkness came suddenly to life with the call of a tawny owl in Burrs Wood, in the little valley below the lane.

March

Spring begins officially on March 21st, but we all have our particular annual symbol representing Nature's rebirth. To many country people the first hearing of the cuckoo signifies that spring is really under way; others wait for the first daffodils, and one man I know never considers that spring has arrived until the silver birch bursts bud and reveals those small, tight, yellow-brown catkins alongside the beautiful crispness of vivid green leaves.

Spring means cleaning, and spring-cleaning on the farm often centres upon the stackyard. Recently I helped to gather together and burn an odd assemblage of relics of bygone days in the stack-yard, near the old cruck barn. The wind was blowing in the right direction, away from the hay under the Dutch barn, and we piled all burnables and set fire to them. I was sorry to see many reminders of former days in the country go up in flames and smoke, but there isn't space or time to save and renovate all the things one would like. A green-painted, all-wood pram on delicately balanced leaf springs, an early attempt at a washing machine, a high-backed wooden armchair which once stood in the kitchen, a pair of cart shafts; and on top of these the old butter churn was piled. The branches of fallen trees and old planks soon glowed red, and the heap settled. Then we put on the rest of the junk—a cracked butter bowl and pats, a commode and a phono-graph and part of an old gig, not used for half a century. We did save two antiques. One was a copper meat jack used to hang over the open fire and from which the joint of meat hung down, slowly revolving by means of the clockwork mechanism inside the jack. The other relic salvaged was a knife cleaner. It is a cir-cular wooden contraption with a handle which, when turned, moved numerous brushes within and these cleaned a knife blade placed in a slot on one side. These objects of another, vanished age will be renovated in due course and put in a prominent position.

Spring really seems to have arrived at last, and the soil is drying out well after recent heavy rains. On quick-draining land here-abouts some farmers are already starting to break up the plough-land in preparation for the sowing of spring corn. No dust yet follows the cultivator or the harrows, but that will surely come soon.

Many cereal growers were very worried during the second half of the last century because of the low-priced corn being pro-duced on the Canadian Prairies and in the United States. It was largely through the efforts and genius of Professor Sir Rowland Biffen at Cambridge that their fears were allayed. By crossing an English wheat with a Canadian one he developed the famous 'Yeoman' variety which combined the high yield of English wheat

Pennine shepherd

with the excellent bread-making qualities of Canadian wheat. It is a winter wheat and by this time of the year will be well grown. Unfortunately this early 'Yeoman' did not breed true to type, giving an unreliable crop. Eventually Sir Rowland found a strain which did breed true and gave good quality and quantity of seed and thereafter helped British farmers to compete more equally with the large transatlantic holdings. Today 'Yeoman' wheat has been displaced by more modern and higher yielding varieties, but for a long time many of the cornfields of the Yorkshire Wolds and in the rain-shadow of the Pennines were sown with this pioneer hybrid variety.

The cattle which roamed wild in Bronze and Iron Age Britain were similar in build to deer, being slender with a slim skull. This animal is today called *Bos longifrons* and was probably never domesticated. Cattle brought here by the Romans were very likely the ancestors of the British White Cattle, known, when semi-wild, as Wild White Cattle. There are still a few herds of these beautiful semi-domesticated animals, notably those in Chillingham Park, Northumberland.

It is interesting to note that the famous Studley herd, near Ripon, helped in the foundation of the Shorthorn breed. Thomas Bates was the originator of the Dairy Shorthorn, while the Colling Brothers of Durham developed and built up the breed. Bates developed the dual-purpose strain so popular with modern breeders, and still animals with one of his cattle family names— Duchess, Foggathorpe, Waterloo, Oxford—are in great demand. In 1873, for instance, a Duchess Shorthorn was sold for 8,120 guineas in New York, and another fetched 7,000 guineas. Such was the demand for 'pure blood' at that time.

For a long period the Shorthorn was the most widespread breed in Britain, in both dairy and beef forms, but today it has lost much ground to the British Friesian.

April

The valley below the farm is quiet, though far from silent. The sounds reach a climax at this time of the year when the natural world is at its most active. On any fine evening one can stand and

12

The River Noe below Edale Head—
The Black Peak

pick out the familiar and unchanging sounds coming up from the newly-green woods and fields below. There is the braying of the donkey on land half a mile away, an almost exotic call which comes up to us so clear in any weather conditions. The piercing screech of a peacock follows, and we can imagine him strutting across his river-side lawn, not far from the donkey. Later the busy twittering of the newly-arrived swallows fills the evening air as they search for flying insects, resting intermittently on the overhead wires.

Perhaps the most evocative of all bird calls comes as light begins to fade behind Bank Green; the leisurely song of the cuckoo—first distantly and then quite near at hand at the head of the valley. Then, as night falls, the flock of guinea fowl begin their clamorous evensong from the highest branches at Adamfield Farm, a combination of screams and cackles more reminiscent of witches than birds. With the coming of darkness most sounds die away, but not all. There is still the sudden, menacing voice of a vixen on the prowl in Rose Wood and the electrifying vibrations of bats beneath the great beech trees.

May

There is no piece of music more evocative of spring than Vaughan Williams' "The Lark Ascending"; no music that I know captures the mood of open pastureland or growing corn or vivid green of sycamore and oak more than this. The other evening I crossed the fields on Barlow Common, making for Bole Hill. A meadow pipit rose from the bright leaves of cocksfoot with which the field was sown, and I soon found its nest, containing four, dark-brown eggs. As I proceeded to the top of the Common a lark sang its happy song against the blue sky of evening. Looking back to the east the far land of the coalfield was brightly illumined by the lowering sun, and all looked surprisingly bright and cheerful—one of the joys of spring lighting.

At the top of Bole Hill stands an ancient home shaded by tall elms. Half a century ago it was a dame's school, and numerous older people in this area remember attending it. Bole Hill is quite a common place-name in the north, usually applied to a hill-top site which shows signs of having been hollowed out. This was done in the Middle Ages for the purpose of iron smelting. In the hollow a fire of charcoal was lit and made to roar by the hill-top winds blowing into it. Iron ore was carted up the slope and smelted at the 'bole' or 'hollow'. As coal replaced charcoal as the smelting fuel the 'boles' fell into disuse.

June

The low evening sun shone brilliantly into our eyes out of the north-west as we walked along the crest of the gritstone edge. Below, to our left, the valley lay in deep shade, and the lowing of cows and a dog's barking drifted up to us. Immediately on our left was the steep drop of the gritstone edge itself, varying between 40 and 80 feet.

During the eighteenth and nineteenth centuries stone masons worked hard and long here, manufacturing great millstones from the face of the escarpment. These millstones were taken away to east and west, to corn mills and, more often from here, to the cutlery works of Sheffield, where they were used to grind the cutting edges on knives and scissors. When demand ceased the quantities of finished or partly-hewn millstones were left beneath the edge and can be seen today, decorated by heather, bilberry and bracken. If they were not so heavy I am certain that many would have been taken away as garden decorations.

These days see different activity on the gritstone edges of the Pennines and Peak District. Many hundreds of climbing routes criss-cross places like Stanage and Curbar and Almscliff, near Leeds, and some of them are extremely difficult. In the descending sunlight we, too, had come to climb and in a few minutes had found the proposed route upon the Great Wall.

July

On any still Sunday evening in summer one can walk up on to the Finney Fields above the town and look one way into Derbyshire and the other way into Yorkshire. It is possible at such times to pick out five separate peals of church bells sounding across the fields and woods.

There is the peal of little Norton Church—now in Yorkshire since the county boundary was moved—close to which was born in 1781 Sir Francis Chantrey, destined to become one of the greatest of English sculptors. From the valley directly below us comes the loud peal of Dronfield's bells. There are eight bells in this fine tower, and six of them are old. Numbers One and Two are inscribed with markings showing that they were presented by J. Bright in 1730, and another possesses the foundry mark of Henry Oldfield, cast in 1615. The most interesting is Number Four which contains the foundry mark of Ralph Heathcote. This family have long resided in the Chesterfield area, and it is believed that this bell was cast before the Reformation.

Along the ridge the sonorious bells of Holmesfield's hill-top church sound out clearly, and at a greater distance the many bells in Chesterfield's notable tower, topped by the world famous crooked spire, ring out, coming and going on every air movement. Old Brampton's bells are the last, heavy calls across the wooded valleys which intervene to the west of Chesterfield. To the newcomer the five peals will be difficult to identify, but one old Dronfield bell-ringer could not only pick out the peals quite easily but could state who was "on the tenor bell at Old Brampton tonight".

August

Above the fields at the edge of the moor the lapwings criss-cross in their typically complicated aerial evolutions, calling "p'weet, pee-wit" over the heifers grazing beneath them. The flight of the lapwing lacks the rapid turns and twistings of the dunlin—often referred to as the ox-bird or sea-snipe.

Beyond the last gritstone wall the moor is coming into its own, turning to vivid purple as the heather and ling comes into gorgeous flower. On fine days in late August the gentle undulations of this moor roll into infinity, and only the occasional passing of a nectar-hunting bee or hover-fly and the distant calls of sheep break the silence.

In the distance the moor rises to an edge where rocks are exposed and form a fine crag. Upon the top of this exposure stand three fine tors, great blocks eroded by millenia of frost, rain, wind and sun. During the last century the names of three British battleships were carved on their sides—*Victory, Indefatigable* and *Royal Sovereign*—while close by stands conspicuously Nelson's Monument, a 10-foot pillar of gritstone, once topped by a large ball and looking out over the valley in one direction and over the rolling moors towards Sheffield and the Yorkshire Pennines the other way.

September

As farmers of a century ago would describe it, this is indeed a "snatch-as-best-you-can" harvest. Knotted and twisted oats present probably the greatest headache, for both combine harvester and binder make heavy going of dealing with it when a rare dry spell lasts long enough for corn cutting to be worth while.

If sheaves of oats are stooked damp and then carried to make large stacks they will heat, and both grain and straw will spoil by threshing time. One device that is used in areas where the corn harvest is often late is a timber framework forming a tunnel a yard high. On top of this a small stack of corn is set up, the tunnel allowing adequate ventilation until the sheaves are dry enough to cart to the big stack. Though fewer corn stacks are made nowadays, the same principles underlying their erection hold good. The best base is made of staddle stones (or stone mushrooms) upon which beams are laid. Such a structure stops the lower courses of sheaves getting damp and prevents rats and mice entering the stack. Every inner sheaf should overlap and hold in place the one in front of it, the layers being higher at the centre so that moisture will run to the butt ends of the sheaf and so to the outside.

Rye straw is the best for thatching, being toughest and stiffest. Wheat is the next best, but combined straw is usually useless for this task.

October

A walk through mixed woodland at this quiet time of the year is always rewarding. Even in the cloudiest weather the dying leaves of oak, beech and birch splash vivid hues on floor and sky;

the yellow needles of larch, our only deciduous conifer, convert the tree to a pagoda of gold for a week or more.

Silent are the walks on a still day, silent that is except for occasional, sudden not unfamiliar, sounds—a cock pheasant's 'trumpeting', the sleepy song of hedgesparrow and wood pigeon, and a dog fox's wail at evening. But if the wood near home is quiet it has many autumnal smells; of the fox, dying bracken and, the strongest of all, the weird stinkhorn. This fungus (*phallus impudicus*) is well named, for the white 'horn' or receptacle bursts upwards with a spore-bearing cap at its end and emits a very pungent smell. One is immediately aware of the stinkhorn when walking in autumn woodland because of the strong odour, resembling to a remarkable degree the smell of bad meat. Unlike most fungi this species does not rely upon wind to distribute its spores but on carrion-loving flies, which are naturally attracted by the strong meat-like smell. Soon the spore-mass at the 'horn's' tip is reduced to a fine lace-like network by the visits of these voracious insects, and the unique fungus loses its 'stink', and later its 'horn'.

October has long been considered the first month of the agricultural year, the month when it was the common practice in former times to insure farm property and to hire labour for the forthcoming twelve months. In old farming manuals one can read detailed hints on the "procuring of sound labour". Suggestions were given as to what the intending employer should look for in a man. "Great strength, endurance and an honest eye" were three notable essential characteristics listed.

In 1808 it was suggested by a notable agricultural writer that, "as many farmers do not give characters, and it is not always easy to form a quick and correct judgement of the accounts given by individuals who want situations", the employers might have, among themselves only, printed circulating letters containing their signature and giving the man's credentials. If this plan was ever implemented it was never accepted on a nation-wide scale, and, in general, the farmers who attended the annual labour-hirings at the local markets in the month of October had to use their own judgement. Often they were right and hired sound and trustworthy labour; sometimes they had to put up with men of an "inferior type, the outcome of deception on hiring day", with whom they had to be content for twelve months.

November

Britain's largest county is one of our most important agriculturally, too. Many of its claims to fame in the farming world are often overlooked; take, for instance, the fact that it has given its name to a grass and to a pig.

Yorkshire fog (*holcus lanatus*) is not a good grass, for it thrives best on the sour soils of millstone grit and coal measures, the fine, silky hairs on its leaves and stem shining silver in fields where it has established a strong colony. At this time of the year the pink-brown flower heads take away some of the 'fogginess' from which the grass gets its name.

A century ago a group of Yorkshire weavers took up pig keeping as a useful hobby and began the improvement of this class of farm livestock, developing the Yorkshire (or Large White) breed. The best known of this enthusiastic group of weavers was a Keighley man called Joseph Tuley, who exhibited his pig at the Royal Show in 1851. He and his wife kept their pig as a pet more than as an 'economic beast', walking it after dinner each day if the weather permitted, or scratching it if wet. On Saturday night it was washed "after t'maister with soapsuds, and shaved by t'mistress when the judges preferred 'em wi'out hair". Tuley brought the breed to fame and provided us with one half of our breakfast tables' standard dish. In recognition of this a well-known early breeder named his house after one of Tuley's sows, as her litter had paid for its erection!

Then there are the county's dogs. A little more than a century ago West Riding woollen workers developed that lovely and diminutive terrier, the Yorkshire. They used it for ratting and as a general 'earth-dog'—for rabbiting and retrieving ferrets—and at this time it weighed as much as a stone, being called the Broken-haired Scottish Terrier until 1870. Today the Yorkshire Terrier is more of a gentleman, and some specimens do not exceed 3 or 4 pounds in weight and have very long, silken hair.

In the valley of the River Aire, at about the same time as the Yorkshire was being evolved, breeders crossed Otterhounds with black-and-tan wire-haired sporting terriers to produce the largest of the terrier family, the Airedale. This fine dog, weighing as much as 50 pounds, also goes by the names of Bingley Terrier, Waterside Terrier and Wharfedale Terrier and has long been used with success as a guard dog. In the Great War it was the renowned army dog, and many are still employed on the railways and docks.

Our old Airedale had a particular fondness for mice. The word had only to be mentioned and Ferguson would show great excitement, rooting beneath the nearest pile of timber or beneath boxes and roof sheets in the yard. He was a prodigious walker, despite his age, this being partly explained by the typical heavily-boned straight legs and the compact feet.

December

As a substitute for watching live birds and animals in the wild it was the Victorian habit to shoot them and have them stuffed and mounted in cases which were often ornate, sometimes ugly and always fascinating. Today the era of the stuffed and mounted creature is almost dead. The taxidermist is a rare craftsman, who usually works in connection with museums, whereas a century ago he was often to be found carrying on his craft in village, town and city, sometimes alongside another occupation.

I have recently been in the process of disposing of my large collection of stuffed birds and animals which have been acquired over the years in a number of ways. A large attic was almost filled with the many cases, and to go up there beneath the roof in the half-light at dusk was an unusual experience—from the corner a pair of long-eared owls tear at a dying starling which is held under their claws, a guillemot raises its wings and a stag's head looks down. The large dog fox has caught a magpie and holds it with one front paw, feathers stuck to his teeth; a family of golden pheasants stand amongst tall, dead grasses; and a gannet surveys the gloomy room with glass eyes. In another corner is a world of the tropics—a tucan perches with its comical, giant beak, and humming birds hang suspended against a deep blue background.

This magic world of squirrels, rabbits, foxes and birds it is a pity in a way to lose, but by the disposal of it to a museum many more people will be able to share the experience. A few of the creatures have been taken away by boys, and to see their bright eyes as they went away with a corncrake or a brent goose in their arms was to know that such Victoriana would continue to be appreciated.

Early winter in the northern hills can bring wet winds and low clouds and heavy underfoot going. Sometimes, though, November goes out and the last month of the year comes in with heavy snowfall. If this is followed by the lucky chance of anticyclonic conditions the whole moorland world is transformed—

> Blow up, snow
> To those peat crests
> And crust the groughs
> To make an easy stride.
>
> Easy is the stride
> Across the frozen peat,
> Silent is the beck
> At one's feet.
>
> Pennine heights seem high
> Under winter snow,
> But Pennine days are short
> And cottage windows glow
> As we return in winter
> To the cosy dale.

Pale, blue dawns send light over the white watersheds, and with keen anticipation we set out for a wonderful day's exploration of some well-known plateau or steep-sided ridge. It is exploration because no matter how well we know the area the coming of snow makes it a different world, with a different character and charm. If only our Pennine winters were more often like that, with deep snow and healthy high pressure maintaining clear and sunny skies.

One such December day comes to mind as I write, a day which dawned clear as crystal with the low sun sending side-long shadows over the rock-hard crust of piled snow. The plateau rolled away like a permanent snowfield under a cloudless blue, white humps and grey-blue shadows lending some scale. Here at 2,000 feet above sea-level the world was new. I know that plateau very well yet here it was, a completely new territory with all its familiar features hidden under a foot and more of ice and snow. A sudden, distant movement drew my attention to a mountain hare which crossed the snow-field, only just visible in its winter coat of white. With the ptarmigan this is one of the best camouflaged of all upland creatures, though its winter coat makes it conspicuous in mild and snowless periods.

Over to the east the bold spur scattered with huge boulders where gritstone outcrops known as the Grinah Stones, reared in powerful profile. The deep cracks and crevasses between the jumbled blocks were now covered over and simplified, but the view from the top, as always, was spectacular. Away down the Westend Valley one looked to the silent conifers ranged up the lower slopes, larch grey-brown and spruce still green. Beyond this trough the great blue bulk of Kinder Scout blocked the southern horizon like a sperm whale surfacing from an ice-floe sea.

The whole day was spent on the shining plateau and during that time only faint whisps of cirrus cloud rose in the western sky, soon to disperse. By sundown, a pale, duck-egg sundown, the sky was perfectly clear once more. As I gained the valley track near the first conifers I looked back to the Grinah Stones. The silver spur towered utterly silent and could, for all the world, have been a 20,000 feet high giant. Nearer, and above where I stood, the cornices lining the edge of the plateau were poised against the black night sky, caught by the first frosty light reflected by the stars. All night those stars would twinkle silently over the incomparable Pennine country.

INDEX